Marcus Kennedy

Special songs and services No. 2

For primary and junior or intermediate classes

Marcus Kennedy

Special songs and services No. 2
For primary and junior or intermediate classes

ISBN/EAN: 9783337266257

Printed in Europe, USA, Canada, Australia, Japan

Cover: Foto ©Thomas Meinert / pixelio.de

More available books at **www.hansebooks.com**

SPECIAL

SONGS AND SERVICES

FOR

PRIMARY AND INTERMEDIATE CLASSES

BY
MRS. M. G. KENNEDY

———•◦•———

BOSTON, MASS., U. S. A.
W. A. WILDE & CO., PUBLISHERS
25 BROMFIELD STREET

To my Friends and Co-workers

OF

THE PHILADELPHIA PRIMARY TEACHERS' UNION,

AND

THE PRIMARY TEACHERS' CLASSES

AND

JUNIOR ENDEAVOR LEADERS

WHO HAVE SO KINDLY RECEIVED ME AT VARIOUS CHAUTAUQUAS, THIS LITTLE
BOOK OF BAIRNS' SONGS AND SERVICES IS

Affectionately Dedicated.

———————

"Sing on, O children!
Yours are the songs we love.
There's ever a ringing in all your singing, —
An echo from heaven above.
Sing on, sing on!
Dear dreams of the past ye bring;
And angels tarry to heavenward carry
The songs that the children sing."   M. G. K.

SPECIAL
SONGS AND SERVICES.

MOTION SONGS.

MOTION SONG BEFORE LESSON.

E. E. Hewitt.   Wm. J. Kirkpatrick.

1. Let us ¹rise, let us rise, All our ²hearts and ³voic-es blend; To the
2. Soft-ly now, soft-ly now, Let our les-son-prayer be said; Humbly
3. Seat-ed ¹all, seat-ed all, Learn-ing with ²at-ten-tive mind, In God's

³skies, to the skies, May our ⁴songs ascend. Praise to ⁵Him who brings us here, In our
¹bow, hum-bly bow, Ev-'ry lit-tle head. Fa-ther, ²bless Thy truth, we pray, Help us
word, in God's word, Blessing we shall find. Move our ³hands and fin-gers, so ! Fold-ed

Sabbath home so dear, Hand in ⁶hand, hand in hand, In His house we stand.
live it, day by day; In Thy love, in Thy love, Teach us from a-bove.
then, ⁴our arms must go, Teacher dear, teacher dear, Read-y now to hear.

MOTIONS.—*First Verse.* 1. Rise in union. 2, 3. Touch heart, lips. 4. Waft hands higher and higher till fully upraised. 5. Hands pressed together, looking up. 6. Join hands. (Children recite, The title of to-day's lesson is —)
Second Verse. 1. Bowed heads. 2. Clasp hands. (Recite, The Golden Text to-day is —)
Third Verse. 1. Take seats quietly. Touch foreheads. 3. Raise arms, shake hands and fingers. Motion may be varied from time to time. 4. Fold arms. Let the teaching of the lesson follow at once, before the perfect order is at all disturbed.

STORY OF THE RAINDROPS.

E. E. HEWITT.   H. R. PALMER.

MET. ♩ = 104.

1. One day, the lit - tle drops of rain, Dash'd [1]down against my window pane;
2. She told me of   the [7]tossing sea, How ver - y strange it seems to me!
3. The lit - tle raindrops [13]feed the rills, That run in [13]music down the hills,
4. Our Heav'nly [17]Fa-ther, wise and great, All things up - on Thy bid-ding wait;

I thought [2]how ver - y nice 'twould be If   I could know their his - to - ry.
The sun can, [8]by   a might-y law, The   o - cean [9]va-pors upward draw,
And these, in turn, will find the sea; There, for a - while [14]their home will be,
Thy hand leads [18]out the   cir-cling sun, And by Thy will [19]the streamlets run;

And   so, my [3]sis - ter's hand I took, And begged her not to read her book,
Un - til they [9]make the clouds on high, Like sails [10]up-on the deep blue sky;
Un - til they rise [15]in   mist a - gain, To form an-oth - er show'r of rain.
At   Thy command, [20]the wa - ters rise, To   o - ver-spread the [21]sunny skies,

But   tell me, [4]on this rain - y day, How came those drops from far a - way.
But when these [11]dark and heav-y grow, They fall in [12]drops to earth be-low.
Ah,   lit - tle drops! [16]I know you well, Your his - to - ry   I now can tell.
And when Thou [22]see'st best, they fall: Dear Lord, Thy love[22]is o - ver all.

STORY OF THE RAINDROPS. Concluded.

CHORUS.

Pit - ter, pat - ter, ⁵pit - ter, pat - ter, Hear the raindrops fall,

Pit, pat, pit, pat, fall. pat, pit, pat,

Pit - ter, pat - ter, ⁵pit - ter, pat - ter, God has sent them all.

Pit, pat, pit, pat,

List - en, ⁶pret - ty lit - tle flow-'rets, To their gen - tle call,

call, pat, pit, pat,

Pit - ter, pat - ter, pit - ter, pat - ter, Hear the rain-drops fall.

Pit, pat, pit, pat,

MOTIONS.—1. Dashing motion, both hands. 2. Cheek resting on hand, in meditation. 3. Take next child's hand. 4. Arms raised, and lowered with fluttering fingers; rain motion. 5. Snapping fingers. 6. Point to flowers, or ground. 7. Wave motion, both hands. 8. Point up. 9. Hands placed low; slowly raised. 10. Hands moved over head. 11. Form arch. 12. Rain motion. 13. Right arm swung with rippling motion of fingers. 14. Wave motion. 15. Hands placed low, slowly raised. 16. Shake forefinger. 17. Look up. 18. Describe circle. 19. Rippling motion. 20. As before. 21. Arch. 22. Hands clasped, look up.

NORTH, SOUTH, EAST, WEST.

Mrs. M. B. C. SLADE.   H. R. PALMER.

Raise your lit - tle hands, and point them to the north, [2] For that is where the

cold win - try wind comes forth; And rush - ing o - ver val - ley, o - ver

plain and hill, [3] The wind of the north [2] works the dear Lord's will. [4]

SCRIPTURE IN CONCERT.

The North and the South, thou hast created them.— Ps. lxxxix : 12.

Cold cometh out of the North.— Job xxxvii : 9.

NORTH, SOUTH, EAST, WEST. Concluded.

2.

1 Raise your little hands, and point to southward, so, [5]
For that is whence the warm summer breezes blow;
And calling out the blossoms, and the green leaves, too, [3]
The will of the Lord doth the south [5] wind do. [4]

SCRIPTURE IN CONCERT.

Thy garments are warm, when he quieteth the earth by the south wind.—Job xxxvii : 17.
Lo! the winter is past, the rain is over and gone; the flowers appear on the earth; the time of the singing of birds has come.—Song of Sol. ii : 11.

3.

1 Raise your little hands, and point them to the east; [6]
For that is where the sun says the night has ceased;
And from the east advancing all the blue sky through, [7]
The will of the Lord doth the bright sun do. [4]

SCRIPTURE IN CONCERT.

He hath set a tabernacle for the sun; his going forth is from the end of the heaven, and his circuit unto the end of it; and there is nothing hid from the heat thereof.—Ps. xix : 4, 6·

4.

1 Raise your little hands, and point them west, [8] you know,
For that is where at sunset the sun must go;
The moon and stars above us, as they brightly shine,
The long, silent night do the will Divine. [4]

SCRIPTURE IN CONCERT.

He made the moon and stars to rule by night.— Ps. cxxxvi : 9.
Praise ye him sun and moon, praise ye him all ye stars of light.— Ps. cxlviii : 3.

5.

1 Raise your little hands, they soon shall folded rest,
When you have pointed north, [2] south, [5] and east [6] and west; [8]
And east, [6] west, [8] north [2] and south, [6] and wheresoe'er we go [7]
Our hands shall the will of the dear Lord do. [4]

SCRIPTURE IN CONCERT.

The night cometh when no man can work.— John ix : 4.
Whatsoever thy hand findeth to do, do it with thy might.— Eccl. ix : 10.

Repeat the singing of the last stanza.

1. Raise the right hand. 2. Point north. 3. Move the hand to and fro. 4. Fold hands. 5. Point south. 6. Point east. 7. Pass the hand from east to west. 8. Point west. 9. Point up.

MARCHING.

A. H. A.

A. H. A.

March movement; not too fast.

March-ing on, Marching on, In the ar-my of King Je-sus. Marching on,

FINE.

Marching on, Glad-ly now the praise we sing of our glo-rious Saviour King.

Lit - tle hands can work for Je - sus, Lit - tle feet can walk His ways,
Lit - tle hearts can learn to trust Him, Lit - tle ears can hear His call,
Lit - tle lips can tell the sto - ry, Of His grace so full and free.

D.C.

Lit - tle tongues can tell His glo - ry, Lit - tle voi - ces sing His praise
Lit - tle prayers from lit - tle children,—Those He lov - eth best of all.
Oh! that all would love Him tru - ly And His faith-ful sol - diers be.

THE SOWER.

Words by Mrs. M. G. KENNEDY.   Music copyrighted by C. DODWORTH.

1. 'T is in the ¹Bi - ble that we read, A sow- er went forth to ²sow his seed; He
2. As he ⁹sowed, some fell by the way, On hard cold ¹⁰ground, and there it lay; And
3. Some seed, up - on a rock was ¹³flung.And ver - y soon it ¹⁴up-ward sprung; So
4. Some seed a-mong the thorns did ¹⁶fall, Which ¹⁷grew up too, and spoil'd it all; No

flung it ³broad-cast o'er the land, With lib - er - al ⁴heart and o - pen ⁵hand.
it was ¹¹trod-den un - der feet, And ¹²birds of the air, the seed did eat.
lit - tle earth was where it lay, As the sun ¹⁵rose it with- ered a - way.
fruit for ¹⁸God will e'er be found,Where thorns and weeds in - fest the ground.

CHORUS.

Let us sow the Gos-pel seed,On which the hungry ⁶soul may feed; Let us do it with
Chorus for last verse only.
We'll re-ceive the Gos-pel seed, By tak-ing now at-tentive ³⁰heed ; Then in our turn more

loving⁷hand,That it may⁸grow in ev'ry land.
seed we'll sow,That ³¹all the earth God's word may
[know.

5 But ¹⁹other seed on good ground fell,
And ²⁰sun and ²¹rain the seed did swell,
Firm ²¹root it took—first ²²blade, then
ear,
An hundred fold for ²³God did bear.

6 Now let each one that hath an ²⁴ear,
Lend it to ²⁵God and for him ²⁶hear;
In each ²⁷heart, may God's word take root.
²⁸Tongue, ²⁹hands and feet for him bear
fruit.

MOVEMENTS. — 1. Hands open like a book. 2. Left arm curled around for basket, from which take seed with right hand. 3. Fling seed with quick movement of right hand. 4. Hand on heart. 5. Right hand held palm upward. 6. Arms crossed over breast. 7. Both hands held outward. 8. Hands brought together in centre then extended wide. 9. Scatter seed to the right. 10. Palm toward ground. 11. Trend with feet. 12. Bird flight down then up. 13. Fling seed. 14. Raise one finger from low to high. 15. Right hand describe circle from east to west. 16. Sowing movement. 17. Lock fingers of both hands together. 18. Point upward. 19. Sowing. 20. Slanting movement for sun's rays. 21. Patter finger tips on back of seat in front. 22. Point finger downward raising gradually till come to word God (23) when point upward. 24. Hold hand to ear as if listening. 25. Point upward. 26. Same as 24. 27, 28, 29. Point to parts named. 30. Hand on heart. 31. Raise both hands high, bringing them down in wide circle.

SEE, OH, SEE!

Words by Mrs. M. B. C. Slade.   Music by W. O. Perkins.

See, oh, see, as here we stand; High we lift each good right hand![1]

Fa - ther, hold our hand, we pray, Help us up the heav'n-ly way.[2]

2.

This the left,[3] and this the right;[1]
We will try with all our might,
Where we turn or where we go,
All His holy will to do.[2]

RECITATION IN CONCERT.

I, the Lord thy God, will hold thy right hand, saying unto thee, Fear not, I will help thee.— Isa. xli : 13.

1. Raise the right hand. 2. Fold the hands. 3. Raise the left hand. 4. Move the fingers of both hands. 5. Hands upon the eyes. 6. Hands upon the ears. 7. Right hand at the mouth. 8. Right hand upon the head. 9. Left hand upon the heart. 10. Lightly work the right foot. 11. Clasp hands, and bow the head.

RECITATION IN CONCERT.

This is the way; walk ye in it: when ye turn to the right hand, and when ye turn to the left.—Isa. xxx: 21.

3.

We will work with either hand,
Swift to do our Lord's command.[1] and[3]
Fingers formed with wondrous skill,[4]
May He teach to do His will.

RECITATION IN CONCERT.

My son keep my words; bind them upon thy fingers; write them upon the tablet of thine heart.—Prov. vii: 3.

4.

Eyes the Lord hath given me,[5]
All His lovely works to see,
Ears that hear what He hath said,[6]
Both of these the Lord hath made.[2]

RECITATION IN CONCERT.

The hearing ear and the seeing eye, the Lord hath made even both of them.—Prov. xx: 12.

5.

Lips and mouth and tongue are these;[7]
And their Maker may they please;[2]
Keep them from each sinful way,
Teach them only truth to say.

RECITATION IN CONCERT.

I will take heed to my ways that I sin not with my tongue.   Set a watch, O Lord, before my mouth; keep the door of my lips.—Ps. xxxlx: cxli: 3.

6.

[8]Head and heart[9] and feet [10] have we;
[11]Father, turn them all to Thee.
Bless Thy children; while they raise
For Thy gift a song of praise.[2]

RECITATION IN CONCERT.

I have refrained my feet from every evil way.—Ps. cxix: 101.
Let thine heart keep my commandments.—Prov. iii: 1.
Blessings are upon the head of the just.—Prov. x: 6.

MORNING, NOON AND NIGHT.

Words by M. B. C. SLADE.   Music by GEO. F. ROOT.

Moderato.

1. Come, hap - py chil - dren, fold each lit - tle hand: [1]What a pleas - ant
2. Rise, [9]lit - tle chil - dren, point-ing to the east; [10]There the morn - ing

sight it is to see our hap - py band. Right,[2]left, [3]up, [4]up,[5]hands and fin- gers
sun ascends[11]when mist-y night has ceas'd. Up, [12]up, [12]on,[13]on,[13]goes the ris - ing

go; [6]Now they clasp a - bove the head,[7]and now we drop them so. [8]
sun, [14]Till we fold our hands [1]at noon when ro - sy morn is done.

3. Turn, [15] merry children, point again so high [14]
   Where the sun at noon-day lights the blue and smiling sky;
   Down, [16] down, [16] on, [17] on, [17] sinking to the west, [18]
   Till we fold our hands [1] at eve, as quietly we rest.

4. Rest, quiet children, [19] lean each little head, [20]
   Just as sleepy children do, before they go to bed.
   Sweet morn, [10] bright noon, [14] sunset, swiftly fly, [18]
   Soon we 'll watch the evening stars that twinkle in the sky. [1]

1. Fold hands. 2. Right hand extended. 3. Left hand extended. 4. Right hand lifted. 5. Left hand lifted. 6. Fingers twirled. 7. Hands clasped. 8. Hands drop by sides. 9. All stand. 10. Right hand points east. 11. Right hand slowly rises. 12. Right hand rises higher. 13 Right hand on from east to west. 14. Right hand points to noon-day sun. 15. All turn south. 16. Hands fall a little. 17. Hands move westward. 18. Point to sunset. 19. Bow heads. 20. Lean heads on hands.

LESSONS FROM THE CLOCK.

E. E. HEWITT.   WM. J. KIRKPATRICK.

1. There ¹stands up - on the land - ing place, A ²great high clock, with ³round, ³round face;
2. Two hands ⁷move on with - out de - lay, And tru - ly tell the time of day;
3. The old clock ⁹has a pleas - ant chime, That clear-ly, sweet-ly, rings the time;
4. Why move ¹¹these bus - y hands so well? Why rings ¹²on time the chim-ing bell?
5. Yes, there's a mainspring out of sight That turns ¹³the lit - tle wheels a - right;
6. If Je - sus rules my ¹⁷heart with - in, And takes a - way the love of sin;
7. So, learn - ing to "re - deem the time," All thro' my life will joy-bells chime,

Let us, in fan - cy, ⁴mount the stair, And learn some use - ful les-sons there.
I have ⁸two hands, are they as true To all the work they have to do?
So let my ¹⁰voice be soft and mild, To speak as should a Chris-tian child.
Is there with - in the clock a pow'r, That keeps it faith - ful ev - 'ry hour?
Then ¹⁴stead-i - ly the weights will go, And not too ¹⁵fast, and not ¹⁶too slow.
My ¹⁸hands will work, my ¹⁹feet will move, My lips ²⁰will speak, as prompts His love.
Oh, ²¹hap - py then the days will be, That draw me, Sav - iour, near - er Thee.

CHORUS.

For the ⁵pen-du-lum, by night and day, ⁶Ticks, ⁶ticks, ⁶ticks, ⁶ticks the hours a - way,
Last verse only.
While the pen-du-lum, etc.

For the pen -du-lum, by night and day, Ticks, ticks, ticks, ticks the hours a - way.

MOTIONS. — 1. Point to supposed landing. 2. Raise right arm, straight and high. 3. Describe circle with hand. 4. Raise right and left feet alternately. 5. Swing right arm across, hanging down. 6. Snap thumb and forefinger. 7. Describe circle with two fingers of right hand. 8. Present hands. 9. Bell motion. 10. Touch lips. 11. Circle with two fingers. 12. Bell motion. 13. Turn both hands rapidly, wheel motion. 14. Lower and raise both arms at the side. 15. Right arms moved rapidly up and down. 16. Left arm moved slowly. 17. Touch heart. 18. Present hands. 19. Take step. 20. Touch lips. 21. Clasp hands, look up.

SCRIPTURE MUSIC.

Words by MRS. M. B. C. SLADE.   Music by H. R. PALMER.

We show you now, with lips and hands, The music of the an-cient bands. We

show you, now, with lips and hands, The mu-sic of the ancient bands.

RECITATION.

Praise Him with the sound of the trumpet; Praise Him with the psaltery and harp; Praise Him with the timbrel and dance; Praise Him with stringed instruments and organs; Praise Him upon the loud cymbals; Praise Him upon the high sounding cymbals; Let everything that hath breath praise the Lord. Ps. cl: 3—6.

2. SONG. The Harp.

‖ : The ten-stringed harp thus David plays,
While this in joyful psalm he says. : ‖

RECITATION.

Upon the harp will I praise Thee, O God, my God. Ps. xliii: 4.

3. SONG. The Organ.

‖ : The organ with their breath they blew,
And touched it, with the fingers, too. : ‖

Sing 1 with folded hands; 2 with left hand extended as in holding the harp, and motions with the right as in playing. 3. The left hand near the mouth as though holding the organ there; the right hand extended as in playing upon it. 4. The two hands arranged as in playing the pipe. 5. Arrange as for playing on the viol, moving the fingers together. 6. Make motions somewhat as in using a tambourine. 7. Meet the thumbs and the ends of the fingers, pointing downward, thus making a triangle. 8. Raise the hands near the mouth as in blowing a trumpet. 9. Make the two hands like hollow cups, then strike them together. 10. Hands as in holding the cornet. 11. Both hands raised. 12. All hands folded. The Scripture Recitations should be in concert.

RECITATION.
Praise Him with organs. Let everything that hath breath praise the Lord.—Ps. cl : 4, 6.

4. SONG. The Pipe.
‖: Thus with their lips the pipe they played,
Their fingers mournful music made. :‖

RECITATION.
My heart shall sound for Moab, like pipes; and my heart shall sound like pipes, for the men of Kir-heres.—Jer. xlviii : 36.

5. SONG. The Viol.
‖: Their fingers o'er the viols went,
And thus sweet melody they lent. :‖

RECITATION.
I will not hear the melody of thy viols. But let judgment run down as waters, and righteousness as a mighty stream. — Amos v : 23, 24.

6. SONG. The Timbrel.
‖: With timbrels beaten till they rang,
Thus Miriam her triumph sang. :‖

RECITATION.
Miriam took a timbrel in her hand: And all the women went out after her with timbrels and dances. And Miriam answered them. Sing ye to the Lord, for He hath triumphed gloriously!—Ex. xv : 20, 21.

7. SONG. The Psaltery.
‖: This is the form, three sides, you see,
Of David's sounding psaltery. :‖

RECITATION.
Sing unto him with a psaltery and an instrument of ten strings; sing unto him a new song, play skilfully with a loud noise. Ps. xxxiii : 2, 3.

8. SONG. The Trumpet.
‖ : With trumpets thus they sounded clear
A blast to call the people near. :‖

RECITATION.
Make thee two trumpets of silver; use them for the calling of the assembly.—Num. x : 2.

9. SONG. The Cymbal.
‖ : Together thus the cymbals strike;
And this is what their form was like. :‖

RECITATION.
Though I speak with the tongues of men and of angels, and have not charity, I am become as sounding brass or a tinkling cymbal. — 1 Cor. xiii : 1.

10. SONG. The Cornet.
‖ : They thus upon the cornet played,
And joyful notes of worship made. : ‖

RECITATION.
With sound of cornet make a joyful noise before the Lord.—Ps. xcviii : 6.

11. SONG.
‖ : Now shall we tell why music rang,
And why their songs of praise they sang? :‖

RECITATION.
The Lord was ready to save me; therefore we will sing my songs to the stringed instruments all the days of our life, in the house of the Lord.—Isa. xxxviii : 20.

12. SONG.
‖ : And this is why their music rang,
And why their songs of praise they sang. :‖

SOWING AND REAPING.

Words by Mrs. M. B. C. SLADE.   Music by H. R. PALMER.

Sow - ing,[1]   sow - ing,   sow - ing the pre - cious seed,

This is the way the seed is sown A - cross the lev - el mead.

RECITATION.

In the morning sow thy seed, and in the evening withhold not thy hand.—Eccl. xi : 6.

SONG.

Growing,[2] growing, growing in sun and rain,
This is the way the seed springs up across the level plain.

RECITATION.

A grain of mustard seed, when it is sown in the earth, is less than all the seed that are in the earth; but when it is sown, it groweth up.— Mark iv : 31, 32.

SONG.

Spreading,[3] spreading, spreading its branches wide;
This is the way the branches spread where singing birds abide.

RECITATION.

It becometh greater than all herbs, and shooteth out great branches, so that the fowls of the air may lodge under the shadow of it.— Mark iv : 32.

Let the class stand. At 1, make, with the right hand, motion for sowing seed. All fold arms during the recitations, which may be in concert, or by a single voice. At 2, let both hands rise with slow, gentle motion. At 3, let both arms stretch slowly to the farthest extent. At 4 and 5, make motions for reaping and binding. At 6, let the class quietly be seated, and rest in silence a quarter of a minute, between song and recitation. At 7, all rise again, and sing more loudly and cheerfully the Praising Song, to the *first* music. The "Trusting" couplet should be sung low and soft. Repeat the praising couplet for closing.

SONG.

Reaping,[4] reaping, thrusting the sickle in;
This is the way the reapers reap, when harvest days begin.

RECITATION.

One soweth and another reapeth. Both he that soweth and he that reapeth may rejoice together.— John iv : 37, 36.

SONG.

Binding,[5] binding, binding the sheaves of wheat;
This is the way they bind the sheaves they bring with joyful feet.

RECITATION.

He that goeth forth and weepeth, bearing precious seed, shall doubtless come again, rejoicing, bringing his sheaves with him.— Psalms, cxxvi : 6.

RECITATION.

Neither is he that planted anything, nor he that watereth : but God, that giveth increase. — 1 Cor. iii : 7.

SONG.

Praising,[7] praising, praising the Lord above,
This is the way we praise the Lord for all His care and love.

RECITATION.

He causeth grass to grow for the cattle, and herb for the service of man; that He may bring forth food out of the earth. I will sing praise to my God, while I have my being. — Psalms. civ : 14, 33.

SONG.

Praising, praising, praising the Lord above, etc.

SPRING SONG.

Words by Eliza E. Hewitt.   Music by H. R. Palmer.

Met. ♪ = 104.
DUET. (*All voices may sing the melody.*)

1. Wel-come, ¹wel-come, sun-ny hours! Wel-come, ²love-ly buds and flow'rs!

ORGAN.

Winds ³that whis-per as they pass To the ⁴dai-sies in the grass,

FULL HARMONY.

Per-fumed breez-es, soft and mild, Tell to ⁵ev-'ry lit-tle child,

This dear les-son of the Spring, God's kind ⁶love in ev-ery thing.

SPRING SONG. Concluded.

All the [7]lil - y - bells are ring - ing, Blossoms on [8]the boughs are swing - ing,

Glad - ly we our [9]songs are bring - ing, For our Fa-ther's name is Love.

2 Brooks are [10]laughing as they run,
 Bright [11]waves shining in the sun,
 Birds are [12]flying thro' the air,
 [13]Beauty — [13]music — everywhere,
 Happy [14]children, look around,
 On fair [15]skies and [16]blooming ground,
 For our [17]Father made them all,
 And He [18]loves us — hears our call.

3 Holy Bible, [19]precious book,
 When on thy [19]dear page we look,
 Better there we read God's love,
 Than in [20]flower or star [21]above.
 Richer than all gifts of Spring,
 Is the gift [22]of Christ our King.
 In Thy garden, Lord, may we,
 Pure and fair forever be.

MOTIONS.—1. Arms extended in welcome. 2. Arms extended downward. 3. Right arm raised, sweeping motion to left. 4. Brought back with sweeping motion to floor. 5. Right hand back of ear, head bent to listen. 6. Arms thrown out. 7. Swing right hand from wrist, arm down. 8. Same, but arm held high. 9. Forefinger touch upper lip, hand wafted upward. 10. Rippling motion of hand, held low. 11. Undulating motion with both hands. 12. Flight motion. 13. Right hand extended, then left, far as possible; brought together with circular motion. 14. Half turn. 15. Look up. 16. Look down. 17. Point up. 18. Fold arms, as embrace. 19. Hold hands together, as open book. 20. Point down. 21. Point up. 22. Raise both arms in praise, looking up.

For Children's Day, or Easter, lilies with a little bell concealed in the flower, may be rung in the chorus.

THE STORY OF RUTH.

(Sung by little girls in white aprons.)

LIDIE E. HEWITT.   DODWORTH.

1. The night's dim,[1] pur-ple shad-ows,   Have part-ed, fold by   fold;
2. "Good-by, good-by, dear[5] mother,"   Hear Ruth, the maid-en,   say,

Forth comes the[2] love-ly Morn - ing, In robes of blue and gold.
As to her field of la - bor, She light-ly [6]steps a - way.

The birds are [3]soar-ing thro' the air, And [4]nod-ing blos-soms ev - 'ry-where,
The field one[7]time by sow-ers sown, Where late the[8]ten-der blades had grown.

MOTIONS.—1. Finger tips together, hands drawn slowly apart, and down. 2. Point to east. 3. Hands as if flying upward. 4. Right hand gently swaying from the wrist. 5. Waving farewell. 6. Stepping forward and backward. 7. As if scattering seed. 8. Hands placed low, then slowly raised. 9. Left hand holding the grain, right hand swinging the scythe. 10. Right hand rotates, as passing line around the sheaves. 11. Tossing motion. 12. Hands fall. 13. Point a little to the right. 14. Hands raised, as in blessing. 15. Heads bowed. 16. Point to distance. 17. As if shaking grain from hands. 18. Bend, and gather supposed handfuls into aprons. 19. Point to west. 20. Stepping with aprons held in both hands. 21. Point to self. 22. Look and point reverently upward.

THE STORY OF RUTH. Concluded.

Now smile a sweet "good-morn - ing," This morning fresh and fair.
There on this sum - mer morn - ing, Ruth hast - ens all a - lone.

3 Each strong and [9] willing reaper
　Is swinging now his scythe,
While cheerily he's singing
　The harvest song, so blythe.
The binders follow in the train,
　See how they [10] tie the sheaves of grain,
And while they [11] toss the [12] bundles,
　Join in the glad refrain.

4 There Boaz stands, [13] the master,
　And scans each busy row,
"God bless you [14] all, my children,"
　(And every head [15] bows low,)
"Who is this modest maiden near?"
　"'Tis Ruth, Naomi's child so dear,
From Moab's [16] distant mountains,
　She comes a stranger here."

5 "Let fall then, for [17] the damsel,
　Some [17] handfuls here and there;
The poor and lonely stranger,
　Must in our bounty share."
So all day long, [18] the maiden bent
　Among the [18] sheaves, in pleased content,
'Til sunset [19] skies were glowing,
　Then home [20] the gleaner went.

6 A nobler field of labor,
　Invites [21] each one to-day;
'Tis [22] Jesus now is calling,
　"Dear children, haste away,"
We'll work for Him with love and prayer,
　He'll help us all our burdens bear,
Then in His Home of glory,
　His blessing we shall share.

LIFT UP!

Words by M. B. C. SLADE.   Music by J. W. TURNER.

Animato.

Lift up, lift up each cheerful voice![1] Like sounding waters sing,   And clap your hands,[2] as they rejoice.[2] And praise the heav'nly King![1] And praise the heav'nly King![1]

RECITATION.

They shall lift up their voice, they shall sing. * * * They shall cry aloud from the sea. — Isa. xxiv: 14.

SONG.

Lift up, lift up[3] your trusting eyes,
To seek our Father's face,
Among the stars,[4] amid the skies, [4]
Behold His dwelling-place. [1]

RECITATION.

Unto Thee lift I up mine eyes, O Thou that dwellest in the heavens. — Ps. cxxiii: 1.

SONG.

Lift up,[5] lift up,[5] our youthful hands!
And bless Him while we live! [5]
Oh, let them do His whole commands, [4]
And willing service give. [1]

RECITATION.

Thus will I bless Thee while I live: I will lift up my hands. — Ps. lxiii:

SONG.

Lift up, lift up to God each heart! [5]
We give them, Lord, to Thee! [3]
Our loving Father, Lord, Thou art,
Thy children let us be!

RECITATION.

Let us lift up our heart with our hands, unto God, in the heavens. — Lam. iii: 40.

SONG.

Lift up your head,[6] and eyes,[3] and voice,
Lift up your hands,[5] and sing!
Lift up your heart, rejoice, rejoice, [2]
And praise your glorious King. [1]

RECITATION.

Lift up your heads, O ye gates, and be ye lift up, ye everlasting doors, and the King of Glory shall come in! — Ps. xxix: 11.

1. Fold hands. 2. Clap hands. 3. Look up. 4. Point upward. 5. Lift both hands.

AN AUTUMN SONG.

E. E. HEWITT.   L. M.

1. Leaves of the Autumn,[1]brown,crimson and gold,   See how they loosen,[2]their
2. Leav - ing the branches that soon will be bare,   Seeking a South [8]Land,all
3. Love - ly the leaves when[6]their time is to fall,   May we like [9]them, when we
4. Hap - py the birds when [5]they leave us to go   To the bright [8]fields never

flut - ter - ing hold,   Whirling,[3]and whirling,[3]and whirling [3]a - round,
sun - ny and fair,   Dear lit - tle birdies, they bid us "good-day,"
hear the glad call,   Put on the garments of glo - ry and praise,
covered with snow;   Hap-py are we, when our Saviour [11]we love,

CHORUS.

Spreading a car - pet [4]all o - ver the ground.   Flitting[5] birds, falling leaves,
Fly-ing, and [5]fly - ing,and fly - ing a - way.
Rob-ing the soul for the Heavenly [10]ways.
Ris -ing to meet Him [10]in Gardens a - bove.

With the garnered harvest sheaves, Tell us that Summer days are past,.Jesus[7]will give us joys that will last.

1. Point to supposed trees. 2. Hands raised, fluttering fingers. 3. Whirl both hands rapidly. 4. Swing arms from side to side. 5. Flight motion. 6. Raise hands and gently lower. 7. Point up. 8. Turn and wave hands toward south. 9. Clasp hands, look up. 10. Both hands uplifted. 11. Hand on heart. N. B. With flight motion in second verse turn southward.

ROBIN'S SONG.

WHISTLING OR HUMMING CHORUS.

Lida E. Hewitt.

J. E. Hall.

Lively.

1. There's a lit - tle [1]rob - in sing-ing, O - ver in the cher-ry tree;

And his mer - ry [2]notes are ring - ing, Ring-ing down to [3]you and [4]me;

And we seem to hear him say, In his hap - py tune - ful way,

Praise the Lord this sun - ny day." Hear the Rob - in's song.

Motions. — 1. Point to supposed tree. 2. Bring down the hand, with spiral motion. 3. Wave to neighbor. 4. Point to self. 5. Lift hands, pressed together. 6. Rain motion. 7. Swing both arms. 8. Fore-finger uplifted; attention! 9. Point up. 10. Flight motion. 11. Same as 2. 12. Touch finger-tips over head, then wave arms apart. 13. Point up. 14. Same as 8.

ROBIN'S SONG. Concluded.

CHORUS.
To be whistled or hummed

2 Still the little robin's singing
    Though the [6] rain-drops quickly fall,
While the [7] leafy boughs are swinging,
    Listen, [8] children, listen, all!
For we seem to hear him say,
    " Though the sunbeams hide away,
Trust in [9] God from day to day."
    Hear the robin's song.
            WHISTLING CHORUS.

3 Now the summer rain is over,
    Robin [10] mounts upon his wings,
Through the [10]air, a joyful rover,
    Still the [11] pleasant carol rings:
And we seem to hear him say,
    " Children, [12] clouds will pass away,
Trust in [13] God, and him obey."
    Hear the [14] robin's song.
            WHISTLING CHORUS.

SEVEN.

Words by M. B. C. SLADE.

Music by FR. W. ROOT.

Allegretto.

One! two! three! four! five! six! seven! [1] Count the love - ly arch of heaven; [2]

Seven bright col - ors make the bow, [3] Bright-est, fair - est thing I know! [2]

See the rain - bow in the heaven; [2] One! two! three! four! five! six! seven! [1]

1.

One! two! three! four! five! six! seven! [1]
Count the lovely arch of heaven; [2]
Seven bright colors make the bow, [3]
Brightest, fairest thing I know!
See the rainbow in the heaven; [2]
One! two! three! four! five! six! seven! [1]

4. RECITATION.

And **God** said, I set my bow in the cloud. When I bring a cloud over the earth the bow shall be seen.—Gen. x: 13, 14.

1. Strike the ends of the fingers upon the desk. 2. Point to the heavens, with the right hand. 3. Mov right hand, uplifted, from right to left. 4. Clasp hands.

2.

One! two! three! four! five! six! seven! 1
Hear the promise God has given : 4
Many troubles I may see,
But the Lord will care for me.
   Hear the promise He hath given;
   One! two! three! four! five! six! seven! 1

4. RECITATION.

He shall deliver thee in six troubles, yea in seven there shall no evil touch thee.—Job v : 19.

3.

One! two! three! four! five! six! seven! 1
Nightly go across the heaven, 3
Seven bright stars, the Pleiades, 2
And the Lord created these. 4
   Nightly go across the heaven, 3
   One! two! three! four! five! six! seven! 1

4. RECITATION.

Seek him that maketh the seven stars, and Orion : the Lord is His name.—Amos v : 8.

4.

One! two! three! four! five! six! seven! 1
Hear the rule of Jesus given; 4
Law of kindness, teaching me
That I must forgiving be.
   Hear the rule by Jesus given;
   One! two! three! four! five! six! seven! 1

4. RECITATION.

If thy brother trespass against thee seven times in a day, and seven times in a day turn again to thee saying, I repent; thou shalt forgive him.—Luke xvii : 4.

LITTLE BUILDERS.

Lidie E. Hewitt.   J. M. Corbin.

1. Lit - tle [1]build-ers all are we, Build-ing for [2]God's eye to see;
2. Lit - tle build-ers, day by day Build-ing with the [11]words we say;
3. Some, a - las! build on the sand, On the drifting, treacherous land;

Not with [3]ham-mer's cheer-y ring, Not with [4]out-ward chis - el - ing;
Build -ing [12]from our hearts with - in, Tho'ts of good or tho'ts of sin.
Ah, when comes [16]the stormy day, Their [17]founda - tions swept a - way,

Back and [5]forth no plane we draw, Nev - er need [6]we use a saw;
Build- ing [13]with the deeds we do, Ac - tions ill, or pure and true;
What than will the build - ers do? Oh, the Word [18]of God is true —

Tho' no [7]tools our hands may show, All the [8]while the build - ings grow.
Oh, how care - ful we must be, Build - ing [14]for e ter - ni - ty.
Lost shall all [19]their life - work be, Lost to all e - ter - ni - ty.

Copyright, M. G. Kennedy.

Motions —1. Building motion, closed fists alternately one above the other. 2. Look and point reverently upward. 3, 4, 5, 6. The motions of the tools mentioned. 7. Present hands, palms outward. 8. Hands placed near floor, and raised slowly. 9. Building motion. 10. Heads bowed, hands clasped. 11. Finger touching lip. 12. Hand on heart. 13. Building motion. 14. Hands pressed together, look up. 15. Arms swung low, fluttering fingers. 16. Arms raised and brought down with fluttering fingers, rain motion. 17. Sweeping motion, with right hands. 18. Point upward. 19. Hands pressed together, brought down with sweeping motion. 20. Step forward, bring feet down very firmly. 21. Arms folded. 22. Point upward. 23. Rain motion. 24. Arms thrown back and forth above head. 25. Hands lightly clapped. 26. Hands put together bowl-shaped. 27. Hand on heart. 28. Building motion. 29. Touch forehead. 30. Touch lip. 31. Hands flung joyfully upward.

CHORUS.

Build - ing, 9 build - ing ev - 'ry day, . .

Help us, 10 Lord, to watch and pray; . .

Build - ing, 9 build - ing, ev - 'ry day, . . .

Help us, 10 Lord, to watch and pray. . .

4 Let us build 18 up on the Rock,
  Firm amid the 20 tempest shock;
  Jesus is the 22 Rock secure,
  Fixed on Him, 21 our hope is sure.
  Though the 23 driving torrent fall,
  Wind to wind 24 in terror call,
  On the solid 21 Rock are we,
  Safe to all 25 eternity.

5 Safe in Jesus, we will sing;
  Precious 26 offerings to Him bring,
  Love's bright 27 gold and silver fair,
  Willing service, faith and pray'r,
  Building to 28 His praise each day,
  All we do, or 29 think, or 30 say,
  Fitting for our Lord to see,
  Temples 31 for eternity.

GOOD-BY SONG.

Words by ELIZA E. HEWITT.   Music by H. R. PALMER.

MET. ♩. = 60. *Don't hurry.*

1. Dear ones[1] all good-[2]by, good-[3]by, Hap - py mo-[4]ments
2. Let us not for - get these hours, May they blos - som[9]
3. Dear ones[11] all good-[12]by, good-[13]by! There's a bless - ed

swift - ly fly, Hap - py mo - ments these we spend,
like the flowers, While from our dear[10] school a - way,
home[14] on high; When we there with Je - sus dwell,

Good - by, ... good -

Learn - ing of the [5]chil-dren's Friend; Dear [6]ones all,
Bear good fruit for ev - er - y day, Dear ones all,
We shall nev - er say, "Fare-well." Dear ones all,

by, ...

Dear ones [7]all, Good - by, good - by, good - by.[8] . . .
Dear ones all, Good - by, good - by, good - by. . . .

MOTIONS.—1. Wave both arms right and left. 2. Bow to the right. 3. Bow to the left. 4. Hands in flight motion. 5. Point up. 6. Bow and wave to right. 7. Bow and wave to left. 8. Bow and wave to teacher. 9. Point down, as to growing flowers. 10. Wave both hands right and left. 11, 12, 13. Same as 1, 2, 3. 14. Hands thrown upward.

RING OUT, MERRY BELLS.

EMILY HUNTINGTON MILLER.   JAMES R. MURRAY.

Joyfully.

1. Ring out, mer-ry bells, in the stee-ple,   Sing loud, hap-py voices, to - night! And
2.   O, nations that wait for the morrow,   Rejoice; for the dawn is at hand! O
3.   The eyes of the blind shall be opened,   The King in His beauty to see; The
4. Ring out, merry bells, in the stee-ple,   Sing loud, happy voices, to - night! And

join with each kin-dred and peo- ple,   In anthems of praise and de- light!
cap-tives who pine in your sor- row,   The Sav-iour shall sev- er your bands!
tongue of the dumb shall be loosened,   To ut - ter its prais-es to Thee!
join with each kin-dred and peo- ple,   In anthems of praise and de - light!

CHORUS.

Good will from the Father a - bove,   Good will to His chil-dren be - low! How

the Father above,   his children below!

glad was the morn When the Saviour was born To ran-som our souls by His love!

THE CHRISTMAS WREATH.

PRISCILLA J. OWENS.   WM. J. KIRKPATRICK.

1. We are lit - tle blos- soms, breathing praise and prayer, Lov-ing words and ac-tions
2. I would be a Rose - bud, smil -ing bright with hope, I would be a Vio - let,
3. I would be a Snow- drop, her - ald of His spring, I would, like the I - vy,
4. I would gather fra-grance in a cup of gold, I would bloom by night His

form our gar-lands fair, Je - sus is our sun-shine, Mak -ing buds complete,
look-ing meek -ly up, I would be a Lil - y, near His heart to rest,
round Him firm - ly cling, I, a blue forget-me-not, faith- ful love would show,
watch-ing to be- hold, I would spread my leaf-lets Where His feet should tread,

D. S. *Bring-ing praise for in - cense, O thou un - de - filed,*

FINE.   CHORUS.

Join our lit - tle hands to make a gar-land sweet. Twin - ing, twin - ing,
I would be a Pan - sy, shin - ing on His breast.
I would be a Dai - sy, in His path to grow.
I would soft-ly twine a - round His man-ger bed.

Join - ing hearts and hands we crown the Ho - ly Child.

Note. — [To be sung by twelve girls. All sing first verse and chorus after each verse. The single lines
of verses 2, 3, and 4 to be sung as solos, each line by one of the girls representing the flower mentioned.
Be careful to have no break between the lines, so that the melody may be maintained as if by one voice.]

THE CHRISTMAS WREATH. Concluded.

D.S.

wreaths and gar-lands sweet, Spreading fra-grant flow'rs at Je - sus' feet.

PRAISES.

EMILY HUNTINGTON MILLER.

GEO. F. ROOT.

Allegretto.

1. Hark the cho - rus swell - ing Thro' the si - lent morn;"Peace in ev - 'ry
2. With the poor and low - ly On the earth He dwelt; Yet the an - gels
3. Stoop-ing in His meek - ness To our path of care; All our pain and
4. Now enthroned in glo - ry, He will stoop to hear, While we tell the

CHORUS.

dwell - ing, Christ, the Lord, is born!" { An - gels may we sing with you?
ho - ly, Low be - fore him kuelt { Glo - ry, glo - ry! let us sing,
weak - ness, His com - pas - sion bare.
sto - ry, Ev - er new and dear.

We have learned the sto-ry too; } Prais-es, prais - es to our heav'nly King!
Prais - es to our heav'n-ly King. }

PRAISE HIM.

J. H. K.   J. H. KURZENKNABE.

1. Light breaks in the east - ern sky— Glo - rious light of proph - e - cy!
2. Him who comes from high- est heaven, Him all praise and love be given,
3. 'Tis of Him the proph - ets tell, He shall rule His peo - ple well;
4. Je - sus, Thou our heart's de-light, Teach us to re - ceive Thee right;

Lo! the Sav - iour prom - ised long Comes announced by an - gel throng.
Ev - 'ry heart a throne pre - pare Fit for Christ to en - ter there.
'Tis Him all the gen - tiles seek, All the world His praise shall speak.
Tune our song that we may bring Wor - thy hon - ors to our King.

CHORUS.

Praise Him, little children, Praise Him, happy children ; Worthy is your Lord and King.

Repeat Chorus pp ad lib.

Praise Him, meek and low-ly, Praise Him, pure and ho-ly, Him your homage gladly bring.

Clap hands in chorus, in time to Music, with sharp sound. Repeat singing and clapping more softly. The Third time, the movement of clapping, but with no sound, while with closed lips the tune is hummed.

CHRISTMAS SONG.

FOR WEEK-DAY FESTIVAL.

Emily Huntington Miller.   Geo. F. Root.

Allegretto.

1. Ho, ho, ho! the wild winds blow; Win-ter is coming, with frost and snow! No
2. Ho, ho, ho! the drift-ing snow   Covers full ma-ny a flower we know; No
3. Ho, ho, ho! our firesides glow,   Making a summer in frost and snow; No

matter—we'll greet him with song and cheer, For jol-ly Saint Nicholas soon will be here.
matter,—the ro-ses will bloom again, To glow in the sunshine and nod in the rain.
matter, tho' skies may be dark a - bove, There's magical light in the eyes that we love.

Chorus.

Ha, ha, ha! we'll sing to-geth-er, In spite of wind and storm - y weather; For

Christmas times are full of cheer, *And Christmas comes but once a year!*

THE BETHLEHEM BABE.
FOR CHRISTMAS.

1. Sweet, sweet, sweet the swell, The swell of Sab - bath bell; But
2. Cold! cold! cold the night, The night was star - ry bright, When
3. Low, low, low the bed, The bed on which His head A-

sweet - er still the notes of praise, The notes of praise our voi - ces raise When
Shep-herds heard the an - gel note, The an - gel note from heav'n a - float, That
mong the beasts was pil-low'd there —Was pil-low'd there 'mid want and care, When

Je - sus' love we're tell - ing, When Je - sus' love we're tell - ing.
told to earth the sto - ry, That told to earth the sto - ry.
God be - came in - car - nate, When God be - came in - car - nate. A - men.

4 Love, love, love unknown !
  Unknown to leave a throne,
  A fallen race from death to save
  From death to save, and in the grave
    To lay His head so Kingly,
    To lay His head so Kingly.

5 Loud, loud, loud we'll raise,
  We'll raise our notes of praise !
  The Bethlehem Babe in manger laid,
  In manger laid, to death betrayed,
    We'll sing, we'll sing for ever,
    We'll sing, we'll sing for ever.

By permission of H. R. PALMER.

HEAR THE MUSIC OF THE BELLS.

L. H. Edmunds,   Wm. J. Kirkpatrick.

1. Hear the music of the grand old bells, Louder still, and louder, on the air it swells,
2. 'T is the sto-ry of the Prince of Peace, Telling of a Kingdom that shall never cease,
3. 'T is a message of the Father's love, Sending down a Saviour from the realms above,
4. While sweet mem'ries of His advent throng, Let us learn the meaning of the midnight song,

Bless-ed is the sto-ry that their chiming tells, Listen to the music of the bells.
Won-der-ful the blessings that shall still increase, Listen to the music of the bells.
Oh, that all the people would His mercy prove, Listen to the music of the bells.
Help to bring the glory that shall come ere long, Listen to the music of the bells,
               mu-sic   of the bells.

Chorus.

O . , , . . the music of the bells,
O the music of the bells, . . . Loud and loud-er how it swells, . .
     O the mu-sic of the bells, Loud . . . . and louder, how it swells,

O . . . . . their
O the story that their chiming tells, Listen to the music of the grand old bells.
            to the mu-sic of the bells.

RING THE MERRY BELLS.

E. E. H.   WM. J. KIRKPATRICK.

1. Ring the mer-ry, mer-ry Christ-mas bells, Ring them far and near;
2. Ring the mer-ry, mer-ry Christ-mas bells, Wake the ju-bi-lee;
3. Ring the mer-ry, mer-ry Christ-mas bells, Thro' the star-ry night,

Peal-ing o-ver hills and dells, Bid the world good cheer.
Hark, the bless-ed mu-sic swells, O-ver land and sea.
Ev-'ry note the day fore-tells, Noon-tide splen-dor bright.

Gold-en hopes and mem-'ries ho-ly, Clus-ter 'round the man-ger low-ly,
Tell the wondrous news from heav-en, "Un-to us a Son is giv-en,"
Christ, the Morn-ing Star is shin-ing, Light that nev-er knows de-clin-ing,

Ring the bells, ring the bells, Ring the mer-ry bells.
Ring the bells, ring the bells, Ring the mer-ry bells.
Ring the bells, ring the bells, Ring the mer-ry bells.

By permission, Wm. J. Kirkpatrick.

RING THE MERRY BELLS. Concluded.

Chorus.

Bells of love, and peace, and gladness, Charm a - way the thought of sadness,
Ring the bells, Ring the bells, Ring the mer-ry, mer-ry Christmas bells,

Ring the mer-ry, mer-ry bells, Ring the mer-ry, mer - ry bells,

Tell a - new the dear old sto - ry; Glo - ry in the high-est, glo - ry;

Ring the bells, ring the bells, Ring the mer - ry bells.

GLORY BE TO JESUS.

E. E. HEWITT.   Chorus by W. J. K.

1. Glo - ry be to Je - sus, Not from lips a - lone, But from hearts sur-
2. Glo - ry be to Je - sus, For His pre - cious blood, Pur - chas-ing our

ren - dered, Now to be His own. Glo - ry, Glo - ry,
par - don, Mak - ing peace with God.

REFRAIN.

Glo - ry be to Je - sus, Glo - ry, glo - ry, Now and ev - er-more.

3 Glory be to Jesus
     For His grace inwrought,
     All our lives transforming,
       Deed, and word, and thought.

4 Glory be to Jesus
     All our ransomed days,
     When He calls us higher,
       His the endless praise.

By permission Wm. J. Kirkpatrick.

RINGING FOR JESUS.

PRIMARY SONG, WITH MOTIONS.

E. E. HEWITT.
WM. J. KIRKPATRICK.

Voices in Unison.

1. Hark! the bells, the Christmas bells, Sweet-ly, sweet-ly ring-ing;
2. I'm so glad that Je-sus came From His home in glo-ry,
3. Je-sus reigns in heav-en now, Yet He hears our sing-ing,
4. Soft-ly lit-tle snow-flakes fall, Rob-ing earth in white-ness;

All the lit-tle ones are glad, Bright-ly, bright-ly sing-ing.
Came a lit-tle child like me, Oh, the love-ly sto-ry!
For He loves us, oh, so well, Takes the hearts we're bring-ing.
So may liv-ing words and ways, Spread their gen-tle bright-ness.

CHORUS.

Ring-ing for Je-sus, mer-ri-ly, mer-ri-ly, Ev-'ry Christ-mas bell;

Sing-ing for Je-sus, cheer-i-ly, cheer-i-ly Children's voi-ces swell.

FIRST VERSE, 1st line.—Right forefingers uplifted, with heads turned as in listening; 2d.—Right arms uplifted, hands swinging from wrists, bell motion. CHORUS, 1st line.—Bell motion. SECOND VERSE, 1st line.—Hands lightly clapped; 2d.—Point up; 3d.—Point to self. THIRD VERSE, 1st line. —Hands together, look up; 4th.—Right hand on heart. FOURTH VERSE, 1st line.—Arms raised, and slowly lowered, with fluttering fingers; 2d.—Sweeping motion toward the earth.

By permission WM. J. KIRKPATRICK.

JESUS LOVES IN HIS ARMS TO HOLD YOU.

A. H. A.　　　　　　　　　　　　　　　　　　　　　　　A. H. A.

1. Lit - tle chil - dren, Je - sus loves In His arms to hold you,
2. If 'tis but a ray of light Cast on path-ways drear - y,
3. Ev - er trust your-selves to Him; He will nev - er leave you:

And with per - fect ten - der - ness, To His bo - som fold you;
Or a kind and lov - ing word Spo - ken to the wea - ry,
Tell Him all your wants and fears, And the cares that grieve you:

Sure - ly, chil - dren, you should love, One so kind and ten - der,
Let your words and ac - tions show, That in you there liv - eth
He will lend a list - 'ning ear, To what-e'er you 're say - ing;

And should try some ser - vice sweet, Ev - 'ry day to ren - der.
One who to each word and deed, Wondrous sweet-ness giv - eth.
Je - sus dear - ly loves to hear Lit - tle chil - dren pray - ing.

CAROLS, BRIGHT CAROLS.

E. E. Hewitt.

Wm. J. Kirkpatrick.

Lively.

1. Car - ols for Eas-ter! Bright songs of the spring, In glad-ness a - ris - ing, Like
2. Car - ols for Eas-ter! Life throbbing a - new, In mead-ow and gar-den, In
3. Car - ols for Eas-ter! A shout for our King; We crown him the vic -tor, Our

Instrument.

birds on the wing: Songs of the sunshine That streams from above; Blos-soms a-waking, Sweet
heav-en's fair blue: Je-sus has ris - en, Al-migh-ty to save; Life is triumphant O'er
glad praises ring: Je - sus has ris-en; Now lift your heads high, Ye gates everlasting; Re-

CHORUS.

hope, faith, and love.
death and the grave.   Car - ols, bright car - ols,   For Him we a-
joice, earth and sky.

dore! . . Liv - ing in Je - sus, Death reign-eth no more.

By permission Wm. J. Kirkpatrick.

MISSIONARY PENNIES.

A Musical Dialogue for two boys and a girl. For Missionary Concerts.

CHARLIE.

1. See here! see here! a bright new cent My fa - ther gave to   me,   ()
2. Oh how I wish I had   a pile Of pen - nies up so high,* What
3. Here,Car - rie, take my bright new cent, I   do not want the   toys;   I 'd

ORGAN.

JOHNNY.

John-ny, say, what would you buy With it   if you were me? And I've a pen - ny,
lots of playthings,love - ly toys,And can-dies I would buy. And I would buy a
rath - er send the Bi - ble to The lit - tle girls and boys. And so would I; take

too, see here! And tho' it is quite small,'Twill buy some can-dy, I   am sure, Or
big live horse,And ride him all the day; I'm sure I nev - er should be tired, Nor
mine a - long And send it, Car-rie, too;   If I'd a pile of pen - nies I Would

* Measuring with his hands.

MISSIONARY PENNIES. Continued.

BOTH.

else a top or ball. Hoo - rah! oh see! A bright new pen-ny for
ev - er want to play. Hoo - rah! oh see! A bright new pen-ny for
give them all to you. ALL. But oh! but oh! 'T is lit - tle that we can

me. Oh, I will buy an él - e - gant toy, A bright new pen-ny for me.
me. Oh, I will buy an el - e - gant toy, A bright new pen-ny for me.
do — So we will send our pennies, dear friend, And leave the dol - lars for you.

CARRIE.

3. Now, boys, if you will listen to me, I 'll tell you something true, I read about some
4. They nev-er have heard of our dear Lord, So gen-tle and so mild, Who blessed the little

MISSIONARY PENNIES. Concluded.

boys and girls A-bout as large as you, They live a-cross the ocean, ma-ny Thousand miles a-
children, and Who loves each lit - tle child. Our people send the precious Word and mission-a -ries

REFRAIN.

way ; They never have read the Bible 'tis said, They never have learn'd to pray. } Oh nay ! they say ! They
there, But ma-ny are lost, so great the cost To keep them ev -'ry year.   }

Da Capo for 5th stanza.

never have learned to pray ;   They never have read the Bible 'tis said, They never have learned to pray.

GOLDEN PENNIES.

Words by E. E. HEWITT.   Music by HENRY BERHARD.

1. Marching, marching, hear the pen-nies chime; Marching, marching, keep good time.
2. Marching. marching, lit - tle fa - ces bright, Marching, marching, foot-steps light.
3. Marching, marching, hear the pen-nies chime; Marching, marching, keep good time.

Lit-tle of-f'rings these we bring To our precious Saviour King; But when given with our love,
Are these pen-nies all we bring To our precious Saviour King? No, our happy songs we raise;
May the gifts we bring to - day, Help poor children far a-way; "Golden pen-nies," wing'd with pray'r,

CHORUS.

He will bless them from a - bove. 1, 2, 3, 4, hear the pennies ring, 5, 6, 7, 8, count them while we sing;
Help us, Lord, to live Thy praise.
Will the news of Je-sus bear.

20,   30,   40,   50, golden pennies make Dollars, given for   the   Saviour's sake.

FREELY GIVE.

AN OFFERING SONG.

E. H.

M. CORBIN.

1. Free - ly give, free - ly give, Hear our bless - ed Sav - iour say,
2. Free - ly give, free - ly give, 'Tis the heav'n-ly Fa - ther's way;

Free - ly give, free - ly give, Gath - ered in His house to - day;
Free - ly give, free - ly give, Mer - cies bright - en ev - 'ry day.

Hap - py praise, hap - py praise, All His grate-ful children sing,
Joy - ful songs, joy - ful songs, Treas - ures from His boun-ty fall,

Hap - py praise, hap - py praise, Will - ing gifts they bring.
Joy - ful songs, joy - ful songs, He has blessed us all.

FREELY GIVE. Concluded.

Free - ly have we all re - ceived, Free - ly give, free - ly give,

Glad - ly now to Je - sus give, Free - ly give.

3. Freely give, freely give,
   Like the golden morning beams;
   Freely give, freely give,
   Like the gaily running streams.
   Blooming flow'rs, blooming flow'rs,
   Yield their sweetness to the air,
   So may we, so may we,
   Do good anywhere.

4. Freely give, freely give,
   Jesus gives His precious love;/
   Freely give, freely give,
   While hosannas ring above.
   "In His name," "In His name,"
   Let us care for those in need;
   "In His name," "In His name,"
   Sow the gospel seed.

GIFTS FOR JESUS.

A. H. A. A. H. A.

1. We are hap-py chil-dren, Cheer-ful-ly we bring To our lov-ing Sav-iour
2. Sing we loud the prais-es Of our Sav-iour King; Well we know He list - ens
3. On-ward, marching onward, "Cheer-ful giv-ers" we. Sending gos-pel sunbeams
4. We will give to Je - sus Lov - ing hearts and true. For the Bi-ble tells us

Now our of - fer - ing. While the gifts are gath-'ring We will march a - long,
To the song we sing. He de-lights to hear us Chant our hap - py strain,
Far a - cross the sea. Gifts of lit - tle chil-dren Can - not be in vain,
This we ought to do. With our gifts, dear Sav-iour, Take our hearts, we pray;

REFRAIN.

And with hap-py voi - ces Sing our of-f'ring song: (May our gifts for Je - sus
As we march, we'll glad - ly Sing our song a - gain:) Light to shine in dark-ness,
Nor the pray'r un-answered Of our sweet re-frain:
Look in love up - on us, Hear us when we say:

1 D S. 2 ritard.

Be in His dear sight Lit-tle gos-pel sun-beams Sending forth the light;
Where'er dark-ness be, Light to lead the erring, (Omit . . . .) Saviour, un-to Thee.

LOVING AND GIVING.

L. E. HEWITT.   C. DODWORTH.

1. Give, lit - tle sunbeams, gold-en-bright; Give' to the world your cheer-y light.
2. Give, pret - ty flow-rets, fresh and fair; Breathing sweet per - fume on the air.
3. Give, lit - tle chil-dren, day by day, Help - ing each oth - er, as you may.

Give, lit - tle wel-come drops of rain, Till thirst - y mead-ows smile a - gain.
Give, lit - tle birds, your spring-time glee, Fill - ing the woods with mel - o - dy.
What can we give our Sav - iour King? Love is the best gift we can bring.

CHORUS.

Giving and lov - ing; loving and giv - ing; So we find the good of liv - ing.

Giving our hearts at our Sav - iour's call; Love is the ver - y best gift of all.

OUR BIBLE SONG.

DAVENANT.

Andantino.

1. How sweet is the Bi - ble! how pure is the light
2. 'Tis the voice of the Sav - iour — how sweet in the storm
3. No words like the words of the Sav - iour, nor can

That streams from its pa - ges di - vine! . . .
It speaks to the sin - ner dis - tressed! . .
Their sweet - ness or val - ue be told: . . . .

'Tis a star that shines soft thro' the gloom of the night,
The tem - pest is hush'd and the sea be - comes calm;
They are words "fit - ly spo - ken" to sor - row - ful man,

Of jew - els a won - der - ful mine. . . . .
The trou - bled and wea - ry find rest. . . .
Like beau - ti - ful "ap - ples of gold." . . . .

OUR BIBLE SONG. Concluded.

'T is   bread   for   the   hun - gry,   't is   food   for   the   poor,
'T is   a   Friend's lov - ing   coun - sel,   the   voice   of   a   guide —
O   teach   me,   blest   Je - sus,   to   seek   for   Thy   face,

A   balm   for   the   wretch - ed   and   sad; . . .
How   gen - tle   and   faith - ful   and   true; . . .
To   me   let   Thy   wel - come   be   given; . .

'T is the gift   of   a   Fa - ther — His   like - ness   is   there,
No   harm   can   the   dear   lit - tle   pil - grim   be - tide
Now   speak   to   my   heart   some   kind   mes - sage   of   grace,

And   the   hearts   of   His   chil - dren   are   glad. . . .
Whose   feet   its   di - rec - tions   pur - sue. . . .
And   words   that   shall   guide   me   to   heaven. .

WHAT LAMPS DO YOU BEAR?

Eliza E. Hewitt.   H. R. Palmer, 1891.

M. 63 =

Girls.*

1. What lamp do you bear, lit - tle pil - grim, To
2. What sword do you need, lit - tle pil - grim, To

3. What food do you need lit - tle pil - grim, What

light - en your path as you go? What light guides your footsteps so
con - quer a - mid the world's strife? What weap - on will give you the

heav - en - ly bread day by day? What man - na fresh gath-ered each

tru - ly, . . With stead - y and beau - ti - ful glow?
vic - t'ry, . . In fight - ing the bat - tle of life?

morn - ing, . . To strength-en your soul on the way?

Boys.*

The lamp I must al - ways bear, And use it with grate - ful
The sword I must ev - er wield And use it with faith's strong

The food that I need each day, The man - na no price can

*For a public occasion, the Lamp, Sword, Staff, Bible, may be held.
Copyright, 1901, by H. R. Palmer and M. G. Kennedy.

WHAT LAMPS DO YOU BEAR? Concluded.

prayer, | To lead me to man - sions fair, . . | Is the
shield, | 'Twill con - quer in ev - 'ry field, . . | Is the

pay, . . | To strength-en me on my way, . . | Is the

MET. 116 =
ALL.

lamp never fail - ing—God's Word. | Oh the Bi - ble is the light, is the
sword of the Spir - it — God's Word. | Oh the Bi - ble is the sword, is the

Bread sent from Heaven—God's Word. | Oh the Bi - ble is the food, is the

light for me, To guide me, to guide me; The
sword for me, To con - quer, to con - quor; The

food for me, To strength - en, to strength - en; The

Bi - ble is the light, is the light for me, To guide me to mansions fair.
Bi - ble is the sword, is the sword for me, To con-quer in ev - 'ry field.

Bi - ble is the food, is the food for me, To strengthen me on my way.

CHILDREN'S SONG OF PRAISE.

Mrs. R. N. TURNER.   WM. J. KIRKPATRICK.

1. Strains of mu-sic ris-ing To the courts a-bove, Bear our praises up-ward To the Lord of love!
2. Fragrant flow'rs are springing At His blest command, All their grace receiv-ing, From His loving hand!
3. With our fes-tal glad-ness, Ev-'ry eye is bright, With our Father's bless-ing Ev-'ry heart is light!

Tributes glad we're bring-ing, At His feet to lay,   Joyful songs we're singing On this hap-py day!
In this glo-ry shar-ing, Let us hast-en now, Crowns of beauty bear-ing, To a-dorn His brow!
Then with ea-ger voi-ces, Raise the song a-bove, While each heart rejoices, In the Lord we love!

CHORUS.

Praise Him, praise Him, Ev-'ry youth-ful heart! Birds and buds and blossoms Glad-ly do their part!

Praise Him, praise Him, Ev-'ry youth-ful heart! Birds and buds and blossoms Glad-ly do their part!

By permission, Wm. J. KIRKPATRICK.

PRAISE THE LORD! YE HEAVENS, ADORE HIM.

JOHN KEMPTHORNE.   W. J. KIRKPATRICK.

1. Praise the Lord! ye heav'ns, a - dore him; Praise Him, an - gels in the height;
2. Praise the Lord, for He hath spok - en; Worlds His might-y voice o - beyed;
3. Praise the God of our sal - va - tion; Hosts on high His pow'r pro-claim;

Sun and moon, re - joice be - fore Him; Praise Him, all ye stars of light.
Laws which nev-er shall be brok - en, For their guid-ance He hath made.
Heav'n and earth and all cre - a - tion, Laud and mag - ni - fy His name.

CHORUS.

Hal - le - lu - jah! hal - le - lu - jah! Praise the Lord and mag - ni-fy His

name! Hal-le - lu - jah! hal- le- lu - jah! Praise the Lord! His mighty pow'r pro-claim.

THIS IS THE WAY THE MIST GOES UP.

EXERCISE SONG FOR LOYAL LEGIONS.

Words by M. B. C. SLADE.   Music by GEO. F. ROOT.

Allegretto.

1. This is the way the mist goes up, [1] From grass, and leaf, and vi - o - let cup. [1] And
2. This is the way it whirls a-round, [2] And turns to drops that fall to the ground, [3] And

softly, gent-ly ris - ing high, [1] Goes hur - ry - ing o'er the bright blue sky. [2] Mist, mist,
this the way the rushing rain [4] Comes pat-ter - ing o'er the flow'rs a - gain. [4] Rain, rain,

beauti-ful mist! [3] This is the way the mist goes up [1] From grass, and leaf and vi - o - let cup. [1]
beauti-ful rain! [1] This is the way it whirls a-round, [2] And turns to drops that fall to the ground. [3]

3 This is the way the streams and rills [5]
  Go speeding on o'er meadows and hills; [5]
  And this the way, by flowery brink [6]
  We merrily stoop, and gaily drink. [6]
         Stream, stream, beautiful stream! [7]
  Go speeding on o'er the meadows and hills. [5]

4 This is the way we raise our hand, [8]
  And pledge ourselves a Temperance band. [9]
  While showers come down [4] and streamlets run, [5]
  Intemperance we will surely shun. [10]
         Pledge, pledge, beautiful pledge! [10]
  This is the way we raise our hand. [8]
  And pledge ourselves a Temperance band. [9]

1. Hands slowly rise. 2. Hands and fingers shaking. 3. Hands slowly fall. 3. Fingers patter on desks. 5. Hands move swiftly to and fro. 6. Bend the head till lips touch the desk. 7. Hands on the desk. 8. Raise right hand. 9. Raise left hand. 10. All clap hands.

PLEDGE SONG.

Alice Gordon Gulick.
March time.

Arr. from Spanish Royal March.
By Chas. T. Kimball.

1. Nev - er, nev - er, With God's help, I'll nev - er touch, Nor
2. Ev - er, ev - er, With His help, We'll ev - er live, For

taste, Nor han - dle the ac - cur - sed drink.
God and Home and our dear Na - tive Land.

Chorus.

{ This is the pledge that we will keep for - ev - er, In the
{ Nev - er, nev - er, with God's help, we'll nev - er touch, Nor
{ Sweet is the ser - vice of Loy - al Tem-p'rance Le - gion, All u -
{ Ev - er, ev - er, with His help we'll ev - er live For

name of Him who gives the vic - to - ry. }
taste nor han - dle the ac - cur - sed drink. }
ni - ted in our joy - ous tem - p'rance band. }
God and Home and our dear Na - tive Land. }

*In singing the 2d verse the effect will be heightened by transposing to key of A (3 sharps).
From Marching Songs, No. 2. By permission Woman's Temperance Publishing Co.

GOD ALWAYS KEEPS HIS PROMISE.

L. HEWITT.

C. R. DODWORTH.

Allegro.

ff

1. God nev - er breaks His prom- is - es, His word is sure and true, We
2. God knows how ve - ry weak we are, But He can make us strong; If

praise Him for His faith - ful-ness, Let me be faith-ful too. For
I but put my hand in His, He'll safe- ly lead a- long. Fa-

I have prom-ised un - to Him, Nev- er to touch strong drink; I
ther in heav - en, bless Thy child, Oh, hear the pray'r I make; Keep

GOD ALWAYS KEEPS HIS PROMISE. Concluded.

must not i - dly pledge my word, No! I will stop and think.
me from this and ev - 'ry sin. For the dear Sav- iour's sake.

CHORUS.

God al - ways keeps His promise, And I must now keep mine. So,

1

trust- ing in His gra- cious help, The tem-per-ance pledge I sign,

2

gra - cious help The tem - per- ance pledge I sign. . . .

RING-A-LING-LING.

BELL CHORUS.

A. A. G.

ANNA A. GORDON.

Brightly. With sleigh bell accompaniment.

1. Ring-a - ling - ling, Ring-a - ling - ling, Chil - dren's hands are ring - ing the
2. Ring-a - ling - ling, Ring-a - ling - ling, Chil - dren's voi - ces swell the

bells.　　Ring-a - ling - ling - ling,　　temp-'rance bells,　　Glad the
sound,　　Ring-a - ling - ling - ling.　　temp-'rance bells,　　Sing and

RING-A-LING-LING. Concluded.

news their mel - o - dy tells,   Ring-a - ling - ling, temp'rance bells. . .
ring the world   a - round,   Ring-a - ling - ling, temp'rance bells. . .

3 Ring-a-ling-ling, Ring-a-ling-ling,
On we march with fearless feet,
Ring-a-ling-ling-ling, temp'rance bells,
Keeping step to music sweet,
Ring-a-ling-ling, temp'rance bells.

4 Ring-a-ling-ling, Ring-a-ling-ling,
Come and join us, girls and boys,
Ring-a-ling-ling-ling, temp'rance bells,
Share our work so full of joys,
Ring-a-ling-ling, temp'rance bells.

5 Ring-a-ling-ling, Ring-a-ling-ling,
Homes are dark and hearts are sad,
Ring-a-ling-ling-ling, temp'rance bells,
We will work to make them glad,
Ring-a-ling-ling, temp'rance bells.

KEEP THE PLEDGE.

Words by E. E. HEWITT.   Music by HENRY BERHARD.

GIRLS.

Keep the pledge, keep it, boys, When you have signed it, If
BOYS.
Keep the pledge, keep it, girls, Keep it to the let - ter; Each

a - ny laugh at you, Nev - er you mind it.
one who lives a - right, Makes the world bet - ter.

CHORUS.

Keep the pledge, keep the pledge, Look-ing to Je - sus, His
ALL.
Keep the pledge, chil - dren all, Break it, no, nev - er! God,

bless - ed grace a - lone, From dan - ger frees us.
who our help - er is, Keeps truth for - ev - er.

THERE IS A HOLY LAND.

1. There is a ho - ly land called Pal - es - tine
2. There in that ho - ly land, the feet have trod

Round which the Chris - tian heart will ev - er twine.
Of proph - ets, priests and kings, an - gels and God.

Sa - cred each height sub - lime, sa - cred each creep-ing vine,
There A - bram's faith was tried, there Da - vid sung and died,

Sa - cred each scene of thine, Blest Pal - es - tine.
There Christ was cru - ci - fied, in Pal - as - tine.

A SONG OF THE HOLY LAND.

Words by ELIZA E. HEWITT.   Music by H. R. PALMER.

UNISON. MET. ♪ = 112.

1. Beau - ti - ful land, "Ho - ly land," O, in the foot-prints of
2. Beau - ti - ful land, "Ho - ly land," O, in the foot-prints of

UNISON.

Je - sus to stand; "Ho - ly land," Beau - ti - ful land, . .
Je - sus to stand; "Ho - ly land." Beau - ti - ful land, . .

Still may we fol - low Him, love's hap-py band. Beau - ti - ful Beth - le - hem,
Still may we fol - low Him, love's hap-py band. Naz - a - reth, nest-ling a -

Beth - le - hem fair! Pre - cious thy name, for King Je - sus came there;
mong thy green hills, Je - sus once strayed by thy cool, flow - ing rills,

With a good map in view, let a scholar point to the places indicated. The exercise may be varied by short readings, or recitations from the Gospels, bearing on the stanzas.

A SONG OF THE HOLY LAND. Concluded.

Leaving His home in the mansions of light, Came a sweet ba-by, one glad starry night.
Watch'd birds and blossoms, a child just like me, "Ho-ly Child Je-sus," my pattern shall be.

3 Beautiful land, "Holy land," etc.
River of Jordan, while crowds gathered round,
By thy famed waters, the Saviour was found;
Looking upon Him, as John did that day —
Dear "Lamb of God," take my sins all away.

4 Beautiful land, "Holy land," etc.
Cana, Capernaum, cities of old,
Here, in my Bible, true stories are told;
There Jesus came in His wonderful might,
Wrought deeds of mercy, made saddened hearts light.

5 Beautiful land, "Holy land," etc.
Galilee, sparkling with sunbeams one hour,
Darkened the next with the storm's fearful power,
Jesus exerting His glorious will,
Trod thy wild billows, and bade them be still.

6 Beautiful land, "Holy land," etc.
Sweet home of Bethany, peaceful retreat,
Here Mary sat at the dear Master's feet;
O, may my heart be a Bethany blest,
Open to Jesus, my Heavenly Guest.

7 Beautiful land, "Holy land," etc.
Royal Jerusalem, joyful with feasts,
To thy grand temple came people and priests;
Day after day, Jesus lovingly taught,
Palms and hosannas by children were brought.

8 Beautiful land, "Holy land," etc.
Passing the gateway, outside the great wall,
Rises Mt. Calv'ry, He died there for all:
Near is the garden-tomb, where Jesus lay
Till He arose on that blessed third day.
Beautiful land, "Holy land," etc.

OUR BIRTHDAY SONG.

E. E. HEWITT.

H. R. PALMER.

MET. ♩ = 60.

1. Hap - py our birth-days, when we glad - ly bring, Hearts of af - fec - tion
2. Hap - py our birth-days, when the past we see Spark-ling with mer - cies,
3. Hap - py our birth-days when His voice we hear, Try - ing to serve Him
4. Hap - py our birth-days, if each milestone be Near - er the man - sions

to our Sav-iour - King, Lay - ing our gifts be - fore Him while we sing
all His gifts so free; Oh how our Sav - iour loves us, you and me!
bet - ter ev - 'ry year; Think-ing of oth - ers we may help and cheer,
by the crys-tal sea; Near - er the Home Land, where His face we'll see,

CHORUS.
MET. ♩. = 60.

Sing - ing His ten - der love.   Sing - ing His ten - der love,
Sing of His ten - der love!
Sing - ing His ten - der love.
Sing - ing His ten - der love.

trust-ing His care, Hap - py our birthdays are, Shin-ing and fair: Well may our

OUR BIRTHDAY SONG. Concluded.

hands grateful of - fer-ings bring; While with our lips bright ho - san-nas we sing.

A BIRTHDAY HYMN.

E. M. R.   E. M. R.

1. Our   Fa - ther,   we thank Thee,   That all   the   year thro,' Thy

good - ness   hath   blessed her   With   gifts   ev - er   new.

2 We praise Thee for blessings
    Sent down from the sky;
    Thy care was about her
    When dangers were nigh.

3 Our Father, we pray Thee
    Be Thou ever near,
    And oh! do Thou give her
    "A Happy New Year."

GOD CARES FOR ME.

E. E. HEWITT.   C. C. CASE.

1. God cares for ev - 'ry lit - tle bird That flits from tree to tree; He
2. God cares for ev - 'ry lit - tle flower, That grows in beau-ty wild, "Much
3. God cares for ev - 'ry lit - tle star, And lights its gold-en ray; He's
4. God cares for ev - 'ry lit - tle thing, In sky, and air, and sea; And

tells me in His Ho - ly Word, That He will care for me.
more," my Sav - iour says, His power Will guard His lit - tle child.
nev - er from His chil-dren far, He keeps them, night and day.
now my hap - py heart will sing, He'll al - ways care for me.

CHORUS.

He'll care for me I know, Be - cause, be-cause He tells me

so; If I His loving child will be, He'll always, always care for me.

THE SUMMER SONG.

C. W. SANDERS.   A. WEBER.

1. Sum - mer days are com - ing, Win - ter days are gone,
2. Hon - ey - bees are gath - 'ring Sweets from all the flowers —

Mer - ry birds are sing - ing In the flow - 'ry lawn. La la
Ev - er, ev - er bus - y All the sun - ny hours. La la

la, la la la, la la la la, la la la la la la, la.

3 May we learn the lesson
    To be busy, too,
  Ever, ever seeking
    Useful work to do.

4 God, our great Creator,
    Gave these summer days:
  May our hearts and voices
    Join to give Him praise.

By permission.

THE CHURCH-BELL

C. R. BLACKALL.   Rev. E. S. LORENZ.

Not too fast.

1. Bim, bome! bim, bome! Rings the church-bell from the stee - ple:
2. Bim, bome! bim, bome! Rings the bell out from the stee - ple;
3. Bim, bome! bim, bome! Loud rings the bell from the stee - ple;

FINE.

Bim, bome! bim, bome! Call - ing to meet - ing the peo - ple;
Bim, bome! bim, bome! Wel - come it gives all the peo - ple;
Bim, bome! bim, bome! Cheer - i - ly call - ing the peo - ple;

Min - is - ter there, Read - y for pray'r, Looking for all of his peo - ple;
We must be there, Bless-ing to share; Room there for all lit - tle peo - ple;
Christians are there, Free from all care: They are the hap-pi-est peo - ple;

D. C.

Sing-ers in place, Fill-ing their space, While rings the bell in the stee - ple.
Songs we may raise, Full of sweet praise; Rings the church-bell from the stee - ple.
Prais-es they sing, Worship they bring; Rings the church-bell from the stee - ple.

By permission.

JOIN THE GLAD SONG.

C. R. Blackall.   H. R. Palmer.

1. Come,   come,   join in the sing-ing, Come,   come,   prais-es are ring-ing, And
2. Come,   come,   join in the sing-ing, Come,   come,   gifts we are bringing, And
3. Praise, praise Him in the sing-ing, Praise, praise sweet-ly is ring-ing, For
4. Come,   come,   join in the sing-ing, Praise, praise sweet-ly be ring-ing, And

joy,   joy,   ev - 'ry heart fill - ing, Makes the full measure of   song. . .
praise, praise, ev - er to Je - sus, Fills all the measure of   song. . .
joy,   joy   com-eth from Je - sus, Fill - ing the measure of   song. . .
joy,   joy,   ev - 'ry heart fill - ing, Rounds the full measure of   song. . .

Fine.

Chorus.

Join . . the glad song, . . And its meas - ure prolong; Oh, come, and now

join . . . the glad song, . . And its beauti-ful measure pro - long. . .

D.C.

By permission.

HOSANNA.

Emily Huntington Miller.
Duet, Soprano and Alto.

Prof. O. Mayo.

1. On His shin - ing throne a - bove, Reigns the Lord of
2. Once His ten - der brow was torn, Pierced by ma - ny a

life and love; While through ev - er - last - ing days, Saints and
cru - el thorn; Now let ev - 'ry lip pro - claim, All the

Softly, and somewhat slower.

an - gels sing His praise; While through ev - er - last ing
hon - or of His name; Now let ev - 'ry lip pro-

CHORUS.

days, Saints and an - gels sing His praise. Chil - dren, come and sing Ho-
claim, All the hon - or of His name.

HOSANNA. Concluded,

san - na; It is meet that you should sing; Once on earth He died to

save you,Now He reigns your glorious King,Now He reigns your glo-rious King!

3 By Thy love that never failed,
    Though the tempter's power prevailed,
Teach our hearts like Thine to live,
    Teach our hands like Thine to give;
Teach our hearts like Thine to live,
    Teach our hands like Thine to give.

4 When our earthly days'are past,
    Gently lead us home at last;
There, through endless days, to sing
    Glory, glory to our King;
There, through endless days, to sing
    Glory, glory to our King.

OUR FATHER IN HEAVEN.

Reverentially.

1. Our Fa - ther in heav - en, We hal - low Thy name!
2. For - give our trans - gres - sions, And teach us to know

May Thy king - dom ho - ly On earth be the same!
That hum - ble com - pas - sion Which par - dons each foe;

Oh, give to us dai - ly Our por - tion of bread:
Keep us from temp - ta - tion, From e - vil and sin,

It is from Thy boun - ty that all must be fed.
And Thine be the glo - ry for ev - er! A - men!

BLESSED ARE THE CHILDREN.

Emily Huntington Miller.

Geo. F. Root.

Andantino.

1. "Bless - ed are the chil - dren!" Hear the Sav - iour's voice;
2. "Bless - ed are the chil - dren! Safe from ev - 'ry snare;
3. "Bless - ed are the chil - dren! They shall sing my praise;
4. "Bless - ed are the chil - dren! In that glo - rious place;

"They that seek me ear - ly, In my love re - joice."
In my arms I fold them, On my bos - om bear."
In my heaven - ly king - dom Sweet - est an - thems raise."
Day and night, their an - gels, See my Fa - ther's face."

CHORUS

Sweet - est songs we sing thee, Loud - est prais - es bring thee!

O - pen wide thine arms of grace, And give thy lit - tle lambs a place.

TO AND FRO, TO AND FRO.

HENRY TUCKER.   HENRY TUCKER.

1. To and fro, to and fro, hear the tread of lit - tle chil - dren,
2. To and fro, to and fro, hear the tread of lit - tle chil - dren,
3. To and fro, to and fro, hear the tread of lit - tle chil - dren,

As they go, as they go; bus - y march of bus - y feet!
As they go, as they go; bus - y march of bus - y feet!
As they go, as they go; bus - y march of bus - y feet!

Here and there, ev - 'ry - where, joy - ous songs we're sing - ing;
We will tell, we will tell, of the won-drous sto - ry,
Thro' the world, thro' the world, do - ing an - gels' du - ty,

Loud and clear, full of cheer, hap - py tones are ring - ing.
While we raise songs of praise to our Lord in glo - ry.
Bright and fair, bright and fair, clothed in an - gel beau - ty.

From " Laudes Domini for the Sunday School." By permission.

TO AND FRO, TO AND FRO. Concluded.

REFRAIN.

To and fro, to and fro, hear the tread of lit - tle chil - dren,

As they go, as they go; bus - y march of bus - y feet!

GOD FOR US.

C. C. C.

CORNET OR BUGLE PRELUDE.

CHARLES CROZAT CONVERSE.

f Spiritedly.

f Spiritedly. March style.

1. God for us,—Our na-tion's hope is sure; God for us,—Our na - tion
2. Hand in hand We form the na-tion's bounds; God for us, The na-tion's
3. God for us,—Our un-ion e'er shall be, Peace, good - will, A true fra-

f

By permission.

GOD FOR US. Concluded.

shall en - dure.   His the praise For our pros-per - i - ty;   His for
song re - sounds. With one flag O'er land and lake and sea; One in
ter - ni - ty.   Un-ion's might, When God the lead-er is, Wins for

peace, and for u - ni - ty.   North and South and East and West,
heart, one in lib - er - ty.
free - dom all vic - to - ries.

Sing God and Un - ion, Home and Lib - er - ty. God for us.

ff Chorus.

ff

f Cornet or Bugle Interlude.

f

JESUS, THOU DRAWEST VERY NEAR.

A. H. A.   A. H. A.

1. Je - sus, Thou draw - est ve - ry near To chil-dren when they pray, And
2. Fill Thou our lives with peace and joy, Teach Thou our lips to sing; If
3. We ask Thee not that all our way, Be strewn with ros - es bright, That
4. So faith- ful to Thee, O our King! Our hearts will ev - er be, For

Thou in love art list - en - ing To all that they may say. Be -
taught by Thee, our songs will be A good - ly of - fer - ing. We
ev - 'ry day be free from care, And all our bur - dens light — But
Thou dost live, O Lord! in us, And we, Lord, live in Thee. Thou

fore Thee now we glad - ly bow, With - out a doubt or fear,
love to use our lips in praise, And lift our hearts in prayer
we would ask that on our hearts, Thy im - age we may wear,
art our Help - er ev - 'ry day, Our Shield thro' ev - 'ry night,

And tho' we do not see Thy face, We know that Thou art here.
Wher - e'er we are thro' all the day; For Thou art ev - 'ry - where.
And al - ways feel, O bless - ed One! That Thou art dwell - ing there.
Our Com-fort- er in ev - 'ry woe, Our Guide to heaven-ly light.

WHAT CAN I DO FOR JESUS.

EMILY HUNTINGTON MILLER.   JAMES R. MURRAY.

Earnestly.

1. What can I do for Je - sus! Who died that I might live! I
2. What can I do for Je - sus! The Lord who loved me so! He
3. What can I do for Je - sus! His lit - tle child am I; He

have no pre - cious jew - els, No cost - ly gems to give;
left His throne in glo - ry To suf - fer here be - low!
keeps my feet from fall - ing, He hears my faint - est cry!

My hands are weak to la - bor, But all my earth - ly
I'll list - en when He calls me, I'll live for Him a -
He is my Heav'n - ly Shep - herd, I'll ask Him ev - 'ry

days My lips shall tell His sto - ry, My tongue re - peat His praise!
lone; And since His blood has bought me, I'll give Him back His own!
day To guide me to His pas - tures, And nev - er let me stray!

BABY LOVES JESUS, TOO.

Dedicated to little Dorothea Opdyke, of Plainfield, N. J.

Words and Music by JOHN LANE.

1. In the home where Je-sus is an hon - or'd guest, His presence gives life and
2. Fond mother tells ba-by the sto-ry of old, Of the Babe in Beth-le -
3. Dear ba-by be-lieves, and the prayer repeats, "Now I lay me down to

light; Where ba - by's voice joins in song with the rest,
hem; The Sav-iour re-ceives little ones to His fold, And
sleep;" And Je - sus a watch o'er the little one keeps, While

CHORUS.

Mother's heart sings with de - light. Dear lit - tle ba - by, Jesus loves ba - by,
tender - ly cares for them.
ba- by is fast a - sleep.

Ba-by loves Jesus, too; Dear little ba-by, Sweet little ba-by, Ba-by loves Jesus, too.

By permission of JOHN LANE.

THE NEW YEAR'S SONG.

EMILY HUNTINGTON MILLER.

GEO. F. ROOT.

Allegretto.

1. Come, hearts in whose puls - es the sum - mer is warm, Tho'
2. The Old year was sad with his bur - dens of care, The
3. O, won - der - ful gifts has the hap - py New Year! And
4. And tho' to some heart that is mer - ry and light, He

win - ter be drear - i - ly blow - ing, We'll greet with a car - ol the
New will be tru - er and bright - er; The Old had its griefs for the
smiles at his pres - ence are wak - ing; New joys for the lives that are
comes with a mes - sage of sor - row; We'll laugh as we sing him a

hap - py New Year, To - night, while the Old Year is go - ing.
gay - est to bear, The New Year will make them the light - er.
lone - ly and drear, And hopes for the hearts that are break - ing.
wel - come to - night, And trust to our Fa - ther the mor - row.

CHORUS.

Toll, bells, for the year that has fled! Toll sor - row - ful chimes at his bier! Then

THE NEW YEAR'S SONG. Concluded.

ring for the New in a ju - bi-lant strain, Ring, bells, for the hap - py New Year.

THE SAVIOUR'S CALL.

Mrs. M. G. Kennedy.   T. Martin Towne.

SOLO, or MAIN SCHOOL. *(May be sung to old tune, " Hallelujah ! 't is done," Key of G.)*

1. { Oh, come all ye chil- dren, and give me your love; Your Sav- iour is
   { Stay not till you're old - er, my warn - ing o - bey; Your souls are in

2. { The voice of your Sav- iour, neg - lect not, nor scorn, God's laws you have
   { But Je - sus so loved you that for you He died, For you He was

3. { Oh, list to His plead- ing, the dear pa - tient Lord, Hear now what He
   { "Oh, come to me ear - ly, I'll free - ly for - give, I'll save you and

4. { Then come from the moun - tain, and come from the plain, The loud call re -
   { Go, sound it a - broad, till the whole world shall ring With prais - es glad

REFRAIN, BY PRIMARY CLASS.

wait - ing and calls from a - bove. }
dan - ger, oh, do not de - lay. }
bro - ken in life's ear - ly morn, }
wound- ed, for you cru - ci - fied. }
says in His own bless - ed word, }
keep you, with me you shall live." }
peat un - to oth - ers a - gain, }
prais - es, to Je - sus our King. }

We are com-ing, we are com-ing, We

hear the loud call, We will come to our Sav-iour, Who so loves us all.

JESUS ONCE WAS A LITTLE CHILD.

(A Song for the Little Ones.)

J. R. M.

JAMES R. MURRAY.

Moderato.

1. Je - sus once was a lit - tle child, a lit - tle child like me,
2. Je - sus once was a lit - tle child, and He grew as chil - dren do,
3. Je - sus once was a lit - tle child, He came to us to show

And He was pure and meek and mild, As a lit - tle child should be;
While His moth - er taught Him lov - ing - ly, To be gen - tle, kind and true;
The way to His pure, sweet life a - bove, From our sin - ful life be - low;

He played as lit - tle chil - dren play, The pleasant games of youth,
O - ver the fields of Beth - le - hem, With playmates He did roam,
We must be, and do, and love like Him, Be kind, all e - vil shun,

But He never got vexed if the game went wrong, And He always spoke the truth.
But He never would fret and scold and pout, When His mother called Him home.
And He'll bring us all to His heav'nly home, When our life-work is done.

JESUS ONCE WAS A LITTLE CHILD. Concluded.

REFRAIN.

So, lit - tle chil-dren, let you and I   Try to be like Him, try, try, try.

LITTLE ONE, COME TO ME.

1. Soft - ly, soft - ly, Christ is call - ing, "Lit-tle one, come to me,"
2. "Come when life's fair morn is bright-est, Lit-tle one, come to me,
3. "They that ear - ly seek shall find me, Lit-tle one, come to me,

Hear the sil - v'ry ech - oes fall - ing, Mu - sic sweet the soul en-thrall- ing,
Come while thy young heart is light- est, Come ere thou the Spir - it blight-est,
Let not sin - ful pleasures blind thee, Hast - en ere the tempt- er bind thee,

"Come to me, come to me, Lit - tle one, come to me."
Lin - ger not, lin - ger not, Lit - tle one, come to me."
Come just now, come just now, Lit - tle one, come to me."   A - MEN.

By permission H. R. Palmer.

HAPPY LITTLE SOLDIERS.

E. E. HEWITT.　　　　　　　　　　　　　　　　　　　　C. C. CASE.

1. Hap-py lit-tle sol-diers, Standing [1] for the right,　Je-sus knows [2] how oft-en
2. Hap-py lit-tle sol-diers, By our [4] Cap-tain led;　With sal-va-tion's [7] hel-met
3. Hap-py lit-tle sol-diers, Fighting on-ly sin;　For the field of bat-tle
4. Hap-py lit-tle sol-diers, Marching [4] bravely on,　By the [2] grace of Je-sus,

We will need His might. So He stays be-side us,　All the night and day,
Cov-er-ing the head. Truth [8] shall be our gir-dle, Take [9] the shield of faith,
Is the [11] heart with-in. Here we'll meet tempta-tion, With the [12] Bi-ble sword,
Star-ry crowns are won. There's a Land of Glo-ry, Where we'll see our King,

CHORUS.

He will tru-ly help us, Ev-'ry [3] time we pray. Marching, [4] marching, Happy [4] lit-tle
Righteousness [10] our breastplate, Faithful un-to death!
Heed the voice of Je-sus, In His ho-ly word.
From His roy-al pal-ace, Songs of [13] vict'ry ring.

sol-diers, March-ing, [4] march-ing, Hear the chil-dren sing. Je-sus goes be-

1. Lifting right feet, bring them down very firmly. 2. Point up. 3. Clasp hands, look up. 4. Keeping step. 5. Wave right hands overhead. 6. Raise both arms. 7. Cover head with both hands. 8. Hands at waist. 9. As if carrying a shield, with right hand. 10. Cover breast with left. 11. Hand on heart. 12. Hands forming book. 13. Wave hands.

HAPPY LITTLE SOLDIERS. Concluded.

fore us, 'T is His[5] banner o'er us, Swell the joy-ful cho-rus, Glo-ry[6] to our King.

CHILDREN'S PRAYER.

A. H. A.

A. H. A.

1. Bless - ed Je - sus, Bless - ed Je - sus, Though but lit - tle
2. We would praise Thee, Bless - ed Je - sus, For Thy love and
3. Take our hearts, so young and ten - der, Mould them sweet - ly

chil - dren we, In Thine arms of love re - pos - ing, Now we
con - stant care, For Thy will - ing - ness to hear us When we
to Thy will; That the life that Thou dost grant us, All Thy

seek to wor - ship Thee, Now we seek to wor - ship Thee.
come to Thee in prayer, When we come to Thee in prayer.
pur - pose may ful - fill, All Thy pur - pose may ful - fill.

4 We are not too young to love Thee,
   Nor to serve the Lord Divine;
May our lives, like little sunbeams,
‖ : Ever through the darkness shine. : ‖

5 Shine to guide some other children
   To Thy pure and holy breast,
To Thy arms so strong, yet tender,
‖ : Where the weary lambs may rest. : ‖

CHARACTER BUILDERS.

C. R. DODWORTH.

1. We are build-ing ev-'ry day, In a good or e-vil way,
2. Do you ask what building this, That can show both pain and bliss?

And the structure as it grows, Will our in-most self dis-close,
That can be both dark and fair, Lo, its name is char-ac-ter.

Till in ev-'ry arch and line, All our faults and fail-ings
Build it well, what-e'er you do; Build it straight and strong and

shine; It may grow a cas-tle grand, Or a wreck up-on the sand.
true; Build it clean, and high, and broad, Build it for the eye of God.

Build-ing, build-ing, ev-'ry day; Help us, Lord, to watch and pray.

I AM JESUS' LITTLE LAMB.

A. H. A.   A. H. A.

1. I am Je - sus' lit - tle lamb, There-fore full of joy I am,
2. Tho' I'm but a lit - tle child, Je - sus my dear Shep-herd mild,
3. If my lit - tle heart is sad, Je - sus al - ways makes it glad

Joy to know and feel and see That my Shep - herd lov - eth me.
Free - ly gives me, day by day, Grace to walk the bet - ter way.
With a Fa-ther's kind ca - ress, Rich in love and ten - der-ness.

REFRAIN.

Je - sus is the chil-dren's Friend, Kind and lov - ing to the end.

4 Jesus, I would cling to Thee,
　　Thou art everything to me, —
　Saviour, Shepherd, Friend, and King,
　　All my heart to Thee I bring.

5 Jesus, Saviour, lead me on
　　Till my days of life are gone;
　In Thy presence then above,
　　I will ever sing Thy love.

OUR REDEEMER'S STORY.

A. H. A.

A. H. A.

1. Tell a-loud the Sav-iour's praise, Sing the song of glo - ry;
2. Saints and an - gels sound His praise O'er the hills of glo - ry;
3. Soon we'll join the hosts that raise, O'er the hills of glo - ry,

Let your joy - ful voi - ces raise Our Re - deem - er's sto - ry;
So should we in tri - umph raise Our Re - deem - er's sto - ry;
Our Re - deem - er's wor - thy praise, Tell-ing forth the sto - ry;

How He left His throne on high, And on earth for us did die,—
How in Death's em - brace He lay Till His own ap - point - ed day;
By His Mer - cy and His care, By His in - ter - ced - ing prayer,

All - suf - fi - cient rea - son why We should ev - er praise Him.
Then He cast Death's cords a - way—Sure - ly we should praise Him.
'Tis that such as we are there.— O! how we will praise Him.

OUR REDEEMER'S STORY. Concluded.

Chorus.

Praise His name, Spread His fame, Je - sus, bless - ed Je - sus;

Loud our voi - ces swell the praise Of our Sav - iour Je - sus.

MAY THE GRACE OF CHRIST OUR SAVIOUR.

1. May the grace of Christ our Sav - iour, And the Fa - ther's boundless love,
2. Thus may we a - bide in un - ion With each oth - er and the Lord,

With the Ho - ly Spir - it's fa - vor, Rest up - on us from a - bove!
And pos-sess, in sweet com-mun-ion, Joys which earth can - not af - ford.

PRIMARY ORDER OF SERVICE, No. 1.

ONE BELL, Come to order.

TWO BELLS, Perfect silence.

SILENT PRAYER, Followed by the Lord's Prayer in concert.

SUPERINTENDENT. This is the day the Lord hath made, we will rejoice and be glad in it.

HYMN.

SUPT. Remember the Sabbath day to keep it holy.

SCHOOL. Six days shalt thou labour and do all thy work, but the seventh is the Sabbath of the LORD thy God.

HYMN BY LITTLE ONES.
> Praise Him for the Sabbath day,
> Praise ye the Lord.

SUPT. Who created the world?

SCH. God.

TEACHER. Who made us?

LITTLE ONES. God.

TEACHER. Where is God?

LITTLE ONES. God is everywhere.

SUPT. What is God's best gift to us?

SCH. God so loved the world that he gave his only begotten Son, that whosoever believeth on him shall not perish, but have everlasting life.

SUPT. Who is the Son of God?

SCH. Jesus Christ is the Son of God.

SUPT. When did Jesus come to this world?

SCH. About 1890 years ago.

SUPT. Where was Jesus born?

SCH. In Bethlehem of Judea, as had been foretold by the prophets.

SUPT. How long did he live on earth?

SCH. About thirty-three years.

SUPT. How did he die?

SCH. He was crucified, nailed to the cross.

SUPT. Why did he come to this earth?

SCH. To save sinners.

SUPT. Who of us are sinners?

SCH. All have sinned and come short of the glory of God.

SUPT. How, then, can we be saved?

SCH. By repenting of our sins and believing in Jesus.

HYMN.

> Jesus died upon the tree,
> From my sins to set me free —
> He is my Redeemer.
> Precious love, wondrous love,

> His own life he gave me;
> On the cross of Calvary
> Jesus died to save me.

SUPT. What is meant by repenting of our sins?

SCH. 'Tis not enough to say
> We're sorry and repent,
> And still go on from day to day
> Just as we always went.

> Repentance is to leave
> The sins we loved before,
> And show that we in earnest grieve
> By doing so no more.

SUPT. What is believing in Jesus?

SCH. It is to believe that Jesus is the Son of God, that our sins are forgiven for his sake, that he will give us new hearts, and that if we obey him, he will take us to be with him forever.

SUPT. Why should we believe?

SCH. He that believeth not the Son shall not see life, but the wrath of God abideth on him.

SUPT. Will our sins be forgiven if we repent and believe?

SCH. Jesus hath said: "Him that cometh to me, I will in nowise cast out."

SUPT. What is it to be a Christian?

SCH. To love and obey Jesus.

SUPT. Can little children be Christians?

HYMN.

> Jesus when he left the sky,
> And for sinners came to die,
> In his mercy passed not by
> Little ones like me.

> Did the Saviour say them nay?
> No; he kindly bade them stay,
> Suffered none to turn away
> Little ones like me.

SUPT. Can little children love and obey Jesus?

SCH. If little children really love Jesus, they will try to keep from being angry, they will try to keep from being selfish, they will be honest and truthful, and will do things on purpose to please Jesus.

PRAYER SERVICE.

SCH. The bell has struck its one, two, three; "Be still!" is what it says to me.

SUPT. What is prayer?

SCH. Prayer is asking God for what we want, and thanking Him for what we have already received.

HYMN.

SUPT. For what should we specially pray?

SCH. To have our sins forgiven.

SUPT. What must we do before we pray?

SCH. Before my words of prayer are said
I'll close my eyes and bow my head;
I'll try to think to whom I pray,
And try to mean the words I say.

PRAYER.

Concert Recitations of Golden Texts.

BIRTHDAY OFFERING.

SUPT. How does God wish us to give?
SCH. God loveth a cheerful giver.
SUPT. Does Jesus know what gifts these little ones have brought to-day?
SCH. He does.

HYMN, *Our Birthday Song.* Page 68.

THOSE BRINGING THE OFFERINGS.

Jesus, bless the pennies brought thee,
Give them something sweet to do,
May they help some one to love thee;
Jesus, may we love thee too!

DROPPING THE PENNIES IN THE BOX.

BIRTHDAY PRAYER.

CONCERT RECITATIONS. Twenty-third Psalm, Books of the Bible, Beatitudes, or Commandments.

SINGING.

INTERNATIONAL LESSON FOR THE DAY.

SUPT. The Lord shall preserve thy going out and thy coming in from this time forth and even for evermore.
What time I am afraid I will trust in thee.
SCH. Our Sunday-school is over and we are going home.
Good-by, good-by!
Be always kind and true.

E. J. PECK.

PRIMARY ORDER OF SERVICE, No. 2.

PRAISE SERVICE. At signal, rise and *recite* or sing: —

Saviour, at thy throne we bow,
Do thou come and meet us now;
Let thy blessing, Lord, we pray,
Rest upon our class to-day.

While we learn from out thy Word,
Do thou grant thy Spirit, Lord;
Help us each and every one —
This we ask, through Christ thy Son.

SING, *Praise Him, Little Children.* Page 34.

TEACHER. Enter into his gates with thanksgiving, and into his courts with praise. — Ps. 100 : 4.
SCH. I was glad when they said unto me, Let us go into the house of the Lord. — Ps. 122 : 1.
TEACHER. Praise our God, all ye his servants, and ye that fear him, both small and great. — Rev. 19 : 5.
SCH. O Lord, open thou my lips, and my mouth shall shew forth thy praise. — Ps. 51 : 15.

Praise God, from whom all blessings flow;
Praise him, all creatures here below;
Praise him above, ye heavenly host;
Praise Father, Son, and Holy Ghost.

PRAYER.

TEACHER. The Lord is nigh unto all them that call upon him, to all that call upon him in truth. — Ps. 145 : 18.
SCH. Evening, and morning, and at noon, will I pray and cry aloud. — Ps. 55 : 17.
TEACHER. Seek ye the Lord while he may be found; call ye upon him while he is near. — Is. 55 : 6.
CHANT. The Lord is in his holy temple: let all the earth keep silence before him. — Hab. 2 : 20.

REPEAT SOFTLY.

Oh, let us, when we try to pray,
Not only mind the words we say;
But let us strive, with earnest care,
To have our hearts go with our prayer.

SILENT PRAYER.

PRAYER.

SONG.

RECITATION, on alternate Sabbaths, of *Commandments, Twenty-third Psalm, Beatitudes.*

MOTION SONG.

BIRTHDAY SERVICE. Receiving of Birthday offerings. *Birthday Song.* Page 68.

Birthday Prayer. We thank thee, our Father, that thou has kept during these   years which   has lived, and hast given   so many blessings. Bless   this year also, and as grows taller and older every day, may grow wiser and more and more like thee. May   be just such a child as thou dost wish   to be. We ask for the sake of Jesus who was once a child. Amen.

MISSION SERVICE. God loveth a cheerful giver. — 2 Cor. 9 : 7.
Remember the words of the Lord Jesus, how he said, It is more blessed to give than to receive. — Acts 20 : 35.

SONG, *Golden Pennies.* Page 47.

GOD'S WORD FOR CHILDREN.

TEACHER. Remember now thy Creator in the days of thy youth. — Eccl. 12 : 1.
SCH. I love them that love me, and those that seek me early shall find me. — Prov. 8 : 17.
ALL. Jesus said, Suffer little children to come unto me and forbid them not; for of such is the kingdom of heaven.

CONCERT RECITATION of Golden Texts, Memory Truths, etc., for the Quarter, interspersed with singing of the Lesson Hymns.

SONG. Before Lesson. Page 3.

LESSON TAUGHT. Suffer no interruptions.

LESSON HYMN FOR THE DAY.

CLOSING SERVICE.

PRAYER. Asking for special blessing upon that lesson.

SONG.

TEACHER. The Lord shall preserve thy going out and thy coming in from this time forth, and even for evermore. — Ps. 121 : 8.
SCH. The Lord shall preserve thee from all evil: he shall preserve thy soul. — Ps. 121 : 7.
TEACHER. For this God is our God for ever and ever: he will be our guide even unto death. — Ps. 48 : 14.
SCH. What time I am afraid, I will trust in thee. — Ps. 56 : 3.

Dear Saviour, ere we part,
We lift our hearts to thee,
In gratitude and praise,
For blessings full and free.

Go with us to our homes,
Watch o'er and keep us there;
And make us, one and all,
The children of thy care.

GOOD-BY SONG. Page 30.

Distribution of papers, etc., as children pass out.

M. G. K.

PRIMARY ORDER OF SERVICE, No. 3.

TEACHER. The Lord is in his holy temple.
SCH. Let all the earth keep silence before him.
TEACHER. I was glad when they said unto me, Let us go into the house of the Lord.
SCH. This is the day which the Lord hath made; we will rejoice and be glad in it.
TEACHER. Serve the Lord with gladness.
SCH. Come before his presence with singing.

SINGING.

PRAYER SERVICE. Talk about Prayer. See page 102.

CONCERT PRAYER.

Gentle Saviour, God of love,
Hear us from thy throne above,
While we meet to praise thee here,
In our Sunday-school so dear.
May the lessons taught to-day
Find us ready to obey:
Make us what we ought to be,
Lead thy little lambs to thee.

PRAYER. In simple words and short clauses by the teacher, the children repeating.

SINGING.

A SCRIPTURE RECITATION.

(WITH MOTIONS.)

Sing unto the Lord with thanksgiving; [1]
Sing praises upon the harp unto our God; [2]
Who covereth the heavens with clouds, [3]
Who prepareth rain for the earth. [4]
Who maketh grass to grow upon the mountains. [5]
He giveth to the beast his food.
And to the young ravens which cry. [6] . . .
He giveth snow like wool; [6]
He scattereth the hoar frost like ashes. [9]
He causeth his wind [10] to blow, and the waters
    to flow [11] . . .
Praise ye the Lord. . . .
Both young men and maidens;
Old men and children;
Let them praise the name of the Lord. [12] — Ps.
    147 and 148.

(DIRECTIONS FOR MOTIONS. — [1] Hands raised as
in prayer. [2] Finger tips of left hand represent
strings of harp, touched by fingers of right hand.
[3] Hands raised high, moved from side to represent
clouds. [4] Hands raised high, fingers curved, falling
as raindrops. [5] Arms raised high, finger tips touching, outlining a mountain. [6] Hands placed side by
side, palms uppermost, curved so as to form a
nest. [8] Hands raised, falling slowly, as snow falls.
[9] Hands extended low, representing frost settled
down. [10] Hands extended, moving rapidly from
side to side as wind blowing. [11] Hands placed palm
to palm, extended in front, moving forward from
right to left, as a river flows. [12] Hands raised as in
prayer.)

JESUS COMMANDS.

(Lift one finger for 1, two for 2, etc.)

I'm going to let my two little hands
Help me remember the Saviour's commands;
There are 1, 2, 3, 4, 5, 6, 7, 8, 9, 10.
The first that were sent to the children of men.
1. Thou shalt have no gods but me.
2. Before no idol bend the knee.
3. Take not the name of God in vain.
4. Dare not the Sabbath day profane.
5. Give both thy parents honor due.
6. Hate not, that thou no murder do.
7. Abstain from words and deeds unclean.
8. Steal not, for thou of God art seen.
9. Make not a sinful lie, nor love it.
10. What is thy neighbor's, dare not covet.

Or substitute part of lesson on Commandments. Page 106.

A GIFT SERVICE.

TEACHER. What kind of a giver does God
love?

SCH. **The Lord loveth a cheerful giver.**

TEACHER. What has God given us?

SCH. **God so loved the world that he gave
his only begotten Son.**

TEACHER. What is said about giving and
receiving?

SCH. **It is more blessed to give than to
receive.**

TEACHER. What about the poor?

SCH. **Blessed is he that considereth the poor.**

RECITE IN CONCERT:

Small are the gifts that we can bring,
    But thou hast taught us, Lord,
If given for the Saviour's sake,
    They lose not their reward.

OFFERING, while singing *Offering March.*
Page 8.

OFFERING PRAYER. We thank thee, dear
Jesus, that thou dost allow us the honor of
giving to thee. We take great pleasure in
making this offering. Please accept it and
give it something sweet to do to help on thy
work. For Jesus' sake. Amen.

BIRTHDAY OFFERINGS.*

God in heaven, our loving Father,
    Six long years, by night and day,
Has watched over our friend Nellie,
    When asleep, at work, at play.
May her life be long and happy,
    May God have her heart's best love,
And when life on earth is ended,
    May we meet in heaven above.

MY PLEDGE.

God help me evermore to keep
    This promise that I make —
I will not chew nor smoke nor swear,
    Nor alcoholic liquors take.

Any of the pledges on page 129 may be substituted.

MOTION SONG.

LESSON SERVICE. Recitation of *Golden
Texts.* Review of Previous Lesson. Lesson
taught.

CLOSING PRAYER. Brief, but earnest, asking
for blessing upon the truths taught to-day.

DISMISSAL MARCH. Singing, *To and Fro.*
Page 78.

PARTING WORDS.

SING, OR RECITE SOFTLY:

Now the time has come to part;
    Father, come to every heart:
Go thou with us as we go,
    And be near in all we do.

BENEDICTION.

TEACHER. The Lord bless thee and keep thee.

SCH. **The Lord watch between thee and me,
while we are absent one from another.**

* Change name, years, and sex, to suit scholar
whose birthday you are celebrating.

PRIMARY ORDER OF SERVICE, No. 4.

GREETING.

TEACHER. Good morning (or afternoon).

CLASS (respond).

TEACHER. Keep thy foot when thou goest to the house of God.

SCH. (With Motions.)
Noiseless feet and folded hands,
Eyes that watch our teacher's face,
Prayerful hearts, and reverent tones,
In this dear and holy place;
Hearts in waiting to receive
All our heavenly Father's grace.

SILENT PRAYER.

SINGING.

TEACHER. And they brought young children to Jesus that he should touch them, but his disciples rebuked those that brought them; but when Jesus saw it he was much displeased and said unto them —

SCH. Suffer little children to come unto me and forbid them not, for of such is the kingdom of heaven.

TEACHER. Verily I say unto you, whosoever shall not receive the kingdom of heaven as a little child, shall not enter therein.

SCH. And he took them up in his arms, put his hands upon them, and blessed them.

TEACHER. And it came to pass as he was praying in a certain place one of his disciples said unto him, Lord, teach us how to pray. And he said unto them, when ye pray, say : —

ALL TOGETHER. Our Father, who art in heaven, etc.

TEACHER. And I say unto you, Ask, and it shall be given you, seek, and ye shall find, knock, and it shall be opened unto you.

SCH. For every one that asketh receiveth, and he that seeketh findeth, and to him that knocketh it shall be opened.

TEACHER. O, come let us sing unto the Lord, let us make a joyful noise unto the God of our salvation.

SCH. Let us come before his presence with thanksgiving, and make a joyful noise to him with psalms.

ALL TOGETHER. For the Lord is a great God, and a great King above all gods.

SINGING.

TEACHER. O, come let us worship and bow down, let us bow before our Maker.

ALL TOGETHER. Bow down thine ear, O Lord, hear me, for I am very needy.

PRAYER.

SINGING.

SCRIPTURE RECITATION. Beatitudes, Commandments, or a Psalm.

MOTION SONG.

TEACHER. What is our *Sunday* text?

SCH. Remember the Sabbath day to keep it holy.

TEACHER. What is our Monday text?

SCH. Suffer little children to come unto me, and forbid them not, for of such is the kingdom of heaven.

TEACHER. What is our Tuesday text?

SCH. I love them that love me, and those that seek me early shall find me.

TEACHER. What is our Wednesday text?

SCH. Remember now thy Creator in the days of thy youth.

TEACHER. What is our Thursday text?

SCH. Though your sins be as scarlet, they shall be as white as snow.

TEACHER. What is our Friday text?

SCH. Come unto me, all ye that labour and are heavy laden, and I will give you rest.

TEACHER. What is our Saturday text?

SCH. Love one another.

TEACHER. What has God given us to use for him?

SCHOOL.

Two little eyes, to look to God ;
Two little ears, to hear his word ;
Two little feet, to walk in his ways ;
Two little hands, to work for him all my days ;
One little tongue, to speak his truth ;
One little heart, to give him in my youth.
Take them, dear Jesus, and let them be
Always obedient and true to thee.

Two little feet, to walk the way to heaven ;
Two little hands, for loving labor given ;
Two little eyes, to read God's holy Word ;
Two little lips, to praise the blessed Lord ;
One deathless soul, beaming with love and light ;
So shall we live always in Jesus' sight.

TEACHER. God has given us so much ; what have we brought him to-day?

OFFERING, while the class recites : —

'T is but little we can give,
But our mites we gladly bring ;
Knowing that our blessed Lord
Will accept love's offering.

He who saw the widow's mite,
Hears the pennies as they fall ;
From his throne in yonder sky
Jesus sees and counts them all.

OFFERING SONG. *Gifts for Jesus.* Page 50.

TEACHER. Raises finger with gesture, as when we say hush! as signal for class to say softly:—

> Softly whisper, softly speak,
> Little children, still and meek,
> Hush! and listen, do not play;
> Hear what the teacher has to say.

LESSON TAUGHT.

SINGING.

GOLDEN TEXTS for quarter.

PRAYER.

> As we *raise our hands* toward the sky above,
> We remember God's banner o'er us is love,
> And we *bow our heads* again in prayer,
> Giving ourselves to his loving care,
> May the lesson learned in our hearts sink deep.
> May the Lord between us a loving watch keep.
> May we show this wish, in our work and play,
> That we've learned of Jesus on this holy day.
> We pray thee to take each little hand,
> And lead us all to the better land. AMEN.

JUNIOR OR INTERMEDIATE DEPARTMENT PROGRAM.

GREETING.

SUPT. Good afternoon (or morning), girls and boys.

SCHOOL (rising). **Good afternoon.**

SINGING.

RECITATION. Golden texts or memory chapter.

SINGING.

PRAYER SERVICE. Explanation of one petition of Lord's Prayer, or brief talk on prayer. See page 102,

PRAYER. Closing by chanting Lord's Prayer, page 102; or singing, *Our Father in Heaven,* page 76.

CHURCH ATTENDANCE SERVICE. All who were present at the morning service, rising.

I was glad when they said unto me: Let us go into the house of the Lord.

RECITATION OF SERMON TEXTS for the quarter.

OFFERING SERVICE.

BIRTHDAY OFFERINGS. These are used for flowers for the sick.

SUPT. What did the Lord Jesus say about giving?

SCH. **It is more blessed to give than to receive.**

SUPT. What did God give us?

SCH. **God so loved the world that he gave his only begotten Son.**

SUPT. What did Jesus give us?

SCH. **He loved me, and gave himself for me.**

SUPT. What should we give to him first of all?

SCH. **Ourselves. Paul says of some who sent him money: "They first gave their own selves to the Lord."**

SUPT. Let us also give our money freely;

SCH. **Freely have we all received, freely give.**

SUPT. Cheerfully;

SCH. **For the Lord loveth a cheerful giver.**

SUPT. Regularly;

SCH. **Upon the first day of the week, let every one of you lay by him in store as God has prospered him.**

SUPT. Thanks be unto God for his unspeakable gift.

SUPT. Our offering to-day is for?

SCH. —— ——. (Name object.)

OFFERING SONG. Page 50.

OFFERING PRAYER.

FIVE-MINUTE LESSON:

> Benevolence.
>   The Book we study.
>   The Land of the Book.
>   The Times of the Book.
>   Temperance.

One subject each week.

FIRST SUNDAY IN MONTH. **Benevolence.** Teaching the names of denominational benevolent societies (missionary, etc.), and the special work of each. SING: *Freely Give.* Page 48.

SECOND SUNDAY IN MONTH. **The Book we Study.** Drill on the books of the Bible; exercise in turning quickly to certain books; lesson about the Bible, page 115. SING: *Our Bible Song.* Page 52.

THIRD SUNDAY IN MONTH. **The Land of the Book.** Exercise in Bible Geography, page 119. *Song of the Holy Land,* page 66; or, **The Times of the Book,** a lesson on Bible chronology, may be substituted.

FOURTH SUNDAY IN MONTH. **Temperance.** Pledge exercise, page 125, or any of the temperance questions and answers on page 126. *Temperance Song.* Page 60 or 64.

LESSON SERVICE.

OPENING WORDS. Superintendent of department, introducing lesson, with object, blackboard, or story.

CLASS STUDY.

CLOSING WORDS. By Superintendent.

PRAYER.

HYMN. *May the Grace of God, our Saviour.* Page 93.

SUPT. The Lord bless thee and keep thee.

SCH. The Lord lift up his countenance upon thee, and give thee peace.

MATERIAL FOR VARYING PROGRAMS.

A CHILD'S CREED. No 1.

I believe in God the Father
Who made us every one,
Who made the earth and heaven,
The moon and stars and sun.
All that we have each day
To us by him is given;
We call him when we pray,
"Our Father, in the heaven."

I believe in Jesus Christ,
The Father's only Son,
Who came to us from heaven,
And loves us every one.
He taught us to be holy,
Till on the cross he died;
And now we call him Saviour
And Christ the crucified.

I believe God's Holy Spirit
Is with us every day,
And if we do not grieve him,
He ne'er will go away.
From heaven upon Jesus
He descended like a dove;
And he dwelleth ever with us,
To fill our hearts with love.

NOTE. The music for this Child's Creed is found in *Songs for Little Folks*, page 52.
This should always be accompanied with motions of the hands, either in reciting or in singing.

CHILD'S CREED. No. 2.

We believe in our Father in heaven
Who made the sky, earth, and the sea;
Who heareth the cry of the raven,
And careth for you and for me.

We believe in his Son, the Lord Jesus,
Who loved us when wandering afar;
Who died on the cross to redeem us,
The babe of the manger and star.

We believe in his Spirit, the Holy,
Who giveth our prayers every one;
Who dwelleth in hearts that are lowly —
One God with the Father and Son.

THE BLESSINGS OF JESUS;
OR,
THE BEATITUDES IN RHYME.

Blessed are the poor in spirit —
They God's kingdom shall inherit.
Bless'd are those who for sin sorrow —
They shall have a bright to-morrow.
Blessed are the meek and lowly —
They the earth inherit wholly.
Blessed are the ones who ponder
God's own truth, and for it hunger —
They shall be denied no longer.
The merciful are ever blest —
For of God's mercy they're possessed.
Blessed are the true, pure hearted —
They from God shall ne'er be parted.
Blessed are the kind peacemakers —
Of God's portion they're partakers.
Blessed are the ones who're willing,
In the places they are filling,
To be persecuted even —
Great is their reward in heaven.
Blessed, always bless'd are they,
Who God's Spirit do obey.

BLESSINGS SOUGHT.

An exercise for little ones.

A. —

God bless my little feet —
So they may never stray,
But swiftly, joyfully tread
In the straight and narrow way.

B. —

God bless my two little hands,
Ne'er may they hurt or destroy,
But may they be willing always
For kind and loving employ.

C. —

God bless my two little eyes,
May they be open to see
All that my Father in heaven
Has done for me, even me.

D.—

God bless my two little ears,
  Ready may they be to hear
The voice of the Saviour, who wipes
  Away the penitent's tear.

E.—

God bless my two little lips,
  Let words of prayer and praise,
Let pity and kindness and love
  Dwell on them the rest of my days.

THE FRIENDS OF JESUS.

[Use as a song in the Primary class. Tune: *I want to be an angel.*]

Of all the twelve apostles
  The Gospels give the names:
First, Andrew, John, and Peter,
  Bartholomew and James;
Matthew and Simon, Thomas,
  Were friends both tried and true;
Then Philip, James, and Lebbæus,
  And the traitor Judas too.
They followed Christ, the Master,
  O'er mountain, shore, and sea,
Samaria, Judea,
  And far-off Galilee.

MOTION EXERCISE.

Take my *hands*, dear Jesus, } *Extending.*
  Let them work for thee;

Never let them idle } *Dropping.*
  Or in mischief be.

Let me fold them softly } *Folding.*
  As thy name I speak;

Let me lift them humbly } *Lifting.*
  As thy grace I seek.

Jesus, my hands I *lift* to thee;
I *look* above, thy light to see;
I *list* to hear thy whisper low;
I *wait* that I thy will may know.
I pray thee take me as I am,
Make me, Lord, thy little lamb. **AMEN.**

A PROMISE.

God help me evermore to keep
  This promise that I make!
I will not chew nor smoke nor swear,
  Nor poison liquors take.

I'll try to get my little friends
  To make this promise too;
And every day I'll try to find
  Some helpful work to do.

A CLUSTER OF NEVERS.

Never utter a word of slang,
Never shut the door with a bang,
Never say once that you don't care,
Never exaggerate, never swear,
Never lose your temper much,
Never a glass of liquor touch,
Never wickedly play the spy,
Never, oh, never tell a lie.
Never your parents disobey,
Never at night neglect to pray.

Remember these maxims
  Through all the day,
And you will be happy,
  At work or at play.

JUST A LITTLE.

Just a little song, Lord,
  Sung at mother's knee,
Yet it tells the story
  Of thy love to me;
Heed the childish praises
  That ascend to thee.

Just a little heart, Lord,
  Willing to obey;
Let no fears assail it,
  Shield it day by day,
Fill it with all goodness,
  Make it thine for aye.

Just a little prayer, Lord,
  Whispered day and night;
May sweet angels bear it
  To thy throne of light;
Simple, though its pleading,
  Thou canst hear aright.

WHAT I HAVE.

Two eyes have I, so bright and clear,
With them to seek both far and near,
The birds, the flowers, the bright blue sky,
The waters deep, the sun on high;
The Lord my God gave them to me—
To him belongs whate'er I see.

Two ears have I, here on my head,
With them to hear what makes me glad,
When mother says, "Come here, my child,
Be always truthful, gentle, mild;"
When father takes me on his knee
And says, "My darling, I love thee."

A mouth have I, and well I know
What with the mouth I oft can do:
Can speak, and ask for many a thing,
Can tell my thoughts, and sweetly sing,
Can pray, and praise the Lord above,
And tell him all my care and love.

Two hands have I, both left and right,
To work and pray with all my might;
Two little feet to leap and run
O'er hills and fields in merry fun,
To ramble by the brook so cool,
To go to church and Sunday-school.

A heart have I, that beats in love
For father, mother, God above —
The Saviour dear, so good and mild,
Who seeks the heart of every child.
Know ye who gave this heart of love?
'T was God the Lord, who reigns above.

LITTLE HANDS.

The little hands, God bless them!
Dimpled hands — not very strong;
Made for kisses and for clinging,
Never made for doing wrong.

Little hands may carry gladness
Into lives made dark by care,
Little hands filled full of flowers
Have a welcome everywhere.

Oh, the little hands, God bless them!
Bless them in their mission sweet,
Till they scatter heavenly blossoms
At the gracious Master's feet.

CLOSING HYMN. 8s, 7s.

Now to him that loved us, gave us
Every pledge that love can give;
Freely shed his blood to save us,
Gave his life that we might live;
Be the kingdom and dominion,
And the glory evermore. AMEN.

TUNE: *Battle Hymn of the Republic.*

We're a band of little workers,
In the service of our King,
Our hearts, our hands, our voices,
Our pennies too we bring;
And we'll make the earth beneath us,
And the heavens above us ring,
As we go marching on.

PRAYER SERVICE.

A LITTLE TALK TO TEACHERS.

There is no subject more important, and none on which we make so many mistakes, as this of teaching the children to pray. Take every opportunity of teaching the nature of true prayer. This should be done not only when the regular lesson happens (?) to be one on prayer, but at other times. Have you ever tried little talks of from one to five minutes preceding the prayer? With primary classes this can be made part of the regular exercises. A tiny talk on each clause of the Lord's Prayer from week to week would result in that wondrous prayer being something more than a parrotlike, vain repetition. I once heard an eminent minister say that he would almost as soon see a Roman Catholic counting his beads as a congregation repeating the Lord's Prayer in concert, for so very few of them really prayed it. Shall we not help to make this a real prayer. Shall we not help to make all prayers to the children truer?

The children should be taught to voice their own special needs to the dear heavenly Father. But many of the children in our classes do not come from Christian homes; do not learn to pray at their mother's knee; have never seen their parents bow in prayer. For this reason it is well to teach several of the little prayer hymns, such as are given on pages 105, 106. They are so easily remembered, and often come involuntarily to the mind in after years.

A PRAYER EXERCISE.

TEACHER. What is prayer?

SCH. Prayer is speaking to God.

TEACHER. To whom alone should we pray?

SCH. To the Lord God, who is our heavenly Father.

TEACHER. Why should we pray?

SCH. He is both great and loving. And we can receive nothing except it be given from heaven. (John 3:27.)

TEACHER. Why should worship be part of our prayer?

SCH. He is thy Lord; and worship thou him. (Ps. 45:11.)

TEACHER. Why should we praise God when we pray.

SCH. For the Lord is great, and greatly to be praised. (Ps. 96:4.)

TEACHER. Should thanksgiving enter into our prayers?

SCH. In everything by prayer and supplication with thanksgiving let your requests be known unto God. (Phil. 4:6.)

TEACHER. Why should we confess our sins to God in prayer?

SCH. If we confess our sins, he is faithful and just to forgive us our sins. (1 John 1:9.)

TEACHER. Give one promise that we may claim when we pray.

SCH. He shall call upon me, and I will answer him. (Ps. 91:15.)

TEACHER. Are there any other promises that God will answer prayer?

SCH. There are many promises that, if we pray aright, God will answer.

TEACHER. In whose name should we pray?

SCH. In the name of Jesus, for he says: "Whatsoever ye shall ask the Father in my name, he will give it you." (John 16:23.)

TEACHER. What kind of things can we ask in the name of another?

SCH. Only the kind of things he would ask if he were in our place.

ALL TOGETHER. O come, let us worship and bow down: let us kneel before the Lord our Maker. (Ps. 95:6.)

PRAYER.

THE LORD'S PRAYER.

For Children's Meetings and Intermediate and Primary Departments. One petition may be explained each week, teaching (so far as suits your needs) the portion of this exercise belonging to such petition.

TUNE: Page 76.

Our Father in heaven,
  We hallow thy name!
May thy kingdom holy
  On earth be the same!
Oh, give to us daily
  Our portion of bread;
It is from thy bounty
  That all must be fed.

Forgive our transgressions,
  And teach us to know
That humble compassion
  That pardons each foe;
Keep us from temptation,
  From weakness and sin;
And thine be the glory,
  Forever, Amen.

TEACHER. What are some wrong ways to pray?

FIRST CHILD. To be seen by others, to make them think we are very good.

SECOND CHILD. To repeat words over and over, on purpose to make the prayer long.

THIRD CHILD. To ask for things without caring whether we get them or not.

FOURTH CHILD. To say words without thinking of what they mean.

TEACHER. What did the disciples ask Jesus to teach them?

SCH. Lord, teach us how to pray.

TEACHER. What prayer did he then teach them?

SCH. The one we call the Lord's Prayer.

TEACHER. What three things should we do when we pray?

SCH. We should close our eyes, bow our heads, and fix our thoughts upon God.

TEACHER. Why should we close our eyes?

SCH. That we might not see anything that would take away our thoughts.

TEACHER. Why should we bow our heads?

SCH. As a sign of respect to God.

TEACHER. Why should we fix our thoughts upon God?

SCH. It would not be real prayer if we did not.

TEACHER. Let us do these three things while we truly pray, as Jesus has taught us:

ALL.

Our Father which art in heaven,
Hallowed be thy name.
Thy kingdom come,
Thy will be done in earth as it is in heaven.
Give us this day our daily bread,
And forgive us our debts, as we forgive our debtors;
And lead us not into temptation,
But deliver us from evil.
For thine is the kingdom,
And the power, and the glory, for ever. Amen.

HYMN. C. M.

The Lord attends when children pray,
  A whisper he can hear;
He knows not only what we say,
  But what we wish, or fear.

He sees us when we are alone,
  Though no one else can see;
And all our thoughts to him are known,
  Wherever we may be.

'T is not enough to bend the knee,
  And words of prayer to say;
The heart must with the lips agree,
  Or else we do not pray.

Teach us, O Lord, to pray aright;
  Thy grace to us impart,
That we in prayer may take delight,
  And serve thee with the heart.

TEACHER. What does this prayer teach us to call God?

SCH. Our Father.

TEACHER. What do our earthly fathers do for us?

FIRST CHILD. They feed and clothe us.

SECOND CHILD. They give us homes, and take care of us.

THIRD CHILD. They teach us to do right, and correct us when we do wrong.

FOURTH CHILD. They love us, and pity us.

TEACHER. What does our heavenly Father know?

SCH. We have need of all these things.

TEACHER. If earthly fathers give us such things, what will our heavenly Father do?

SCH. How much more shall your Father which is in heaven give good things to them that ask him.

TEACHER. What gift has our heavenly Father that earthly fathers cannot give?

SCH. How much more shall your heavenly Father give the Holy Spirit to them that ask him?

TEACHER. How should children treat their fathers?

SCH. We should love, honor, obey, serve, our earthly, and still more our heavenly Father.

TEACHER. Then what do these two words, "Our Father," teach us that we may do?

SCH. As his children, we may call on our Father, Lord of all.

> Art thou my Father? Let me be
> A meek, obedient child to thee;
> And try in word and deed and thought,
> To serve and please thee as I ought.

> Art thou my Father? I'll depend
> Upon the care of such a Friend;
> And only wish to do and be
> Whatever seemeth good to thee.

TEACHER. Where does the prayer say our Father lives?

SCH. Which art in heaven.

TEACHER. Is God in heaven only?

SCH. No; he is everywhere; he is here.

TEACHER. Why then do we say, "Our Father which art in heaven"?

SCH. Thus saith the Lord, The heaven is my throne.

TEACHER. What do we first ask in this prayer?

SCH. Hallowed be thy name.

TEACHER. What does hallowed mean?

SCH. Keep holy.

TEACHER. Speak, very softly, some of God's names.

SCH. Jehovah; Holy One; God of Hosts; Mighty God; Most High God; Living God; King of kings and Lord of lords.

TEACHER. How can we help answer this prayer?

SCH. By never speaking God's name carelessly.

SING.

> Holy, holy, holy! Lord God Almighty!
> Early in the morning, our song shall rise to thee;
> Holy, holy, holy! Merciful and mighty,
> God in three persons, blessed Trinity.

TEACHER. What do we next ask?

SCH. Thy kingdom come.

TEACHER. What is God's kingdom?

SCH. His reigning as a king in the heart of his people.

TEACHER. When does he reign thus?

SCH. When we love and obey him.

TEACHER. What do we pray for when we ask, "Thy kingdom come"?

SCH. That all people, everywhere, shall love and obey him.

TEACHER. How can we help to answer this prayer?

FIRST CHILD. By loving and obeying him myself.

SECOND CHILD. By praying for others.

THIRD CHILD. By telling others about Jesus.

FOURTH CHILD. By giving to send Bibles and missionaries to those who do not know about him.

8s, 7s.

> Let thy kingdom come, we pray thee,
> Let the world in thee find rest,
> Let all know thee and obey thee,
> Loving, praising, blessing, blessed!

> Let the sweet and joyful story
> Of the Saviour's wondrous love
> Wake on earth a song of glory,
> Like the angels' songs above.

TEACHER. What do we next ask?

SCH. Thy will be done on earth, as it is in heaven.

TEACHER. What is God's will for us?

SCH. That we should live pure, earnest, Christian lives.

TEACHER. How is God's will done in heaven?

SCH. Gladly, promptly, without asking questions.

TEACHER. How can we help to answer this prayer?

SCH. By trying, with the help of the Holy Spirit, to do only such things as please him.

TEACHER. What do we next pray?

SCH. Give us this day our daily bread.

TEACHER. Why did not this part come before?

SCH. Doing God's will is more important even than that we should be fed.

TEACHER. Of what may we be sure?

SCH. If we do his will, he will feed and clothe us.

TEACHER. Why do we not ask for food for more than this day?

SCH. If we pray every day to be fed this day, we shall always be fed.

TEACHER. What comes next in the prayer?

SCH. **Forgive us our debts, as we forgive our debtors.**

TEACHER. What is here meant by our debts?

SCH. **Our sins.**

TEACHER. Who are our debtors?

SCH. **Those who have done wrong to us.**

TEACHER. How much should we forgive?

SCH. **As God, for Christ's sake, has forgiven us.**

TEACHER. If we pray this, without forgiving others, what do we really ask?

SCH. **To be treated in the same way; that is, that we should not be forgiven.**

TEACHER. What two prayers do we next make?

SCH. **Lead us not into temptation; but deliver us from evil.**

TEACHER. What promise have we, when tempted to do wrong?

SCH. **He is able to succour them that are tempted.**

TEACHER. What did Jesus ask in his last prayer for his people?

SCH. **That thou shouldest keep them from the evil.**

SING.

Ask the Saviour to help you, comfort, strengthen, and keep you.
He is willing to aid you; he will carry you through.

TEACHER. What three things may give us confidence to ask all these things in this prayer?

SCH. **For thine is the kingdom, and the power, and the glory, forever.**

TEACHER. What do even the angels in heaven pray?

ALL. **Amen.**

BOYS. **Blessing, and glory,**

GIRLS. **And wisdom, and thanksgiving,**

BOYS. **And honour, and power, and might,**

GIRLS. **Be unto our God,**

ALL. **For ever and ever. Amen.**

TEACHER. What does Amen mean?

SCH. **So let it be.**

TEACHER. If we say Amen to a prayer, what must we do?

SCH. **We must do all we can to answer it ourselves.**

Hallelujah! Thine the kingdom. Hallelujah! Amen.
Hallelujah! Thine the power, the glory. Amen.

RECITATION.

FIRST CHILD. **Our Father, throned where angels bow,**

SECOND CHILD. **Thy name be hallowed here below;**

THIRD CHILD. **Thy kingdom come;**

FOURTH CHILD. **Thy will be done on earth, as done in heaven;**

FIFTH CHILD. **Give us our bread, each day its own;**

SIXTH CHILD. **And be our sins forgiven, as we forgive the wrongs we bear;**

SEVENTH CHILD. **Our weakness from temptation spare; from evil save;**

EIGHTH CHILD. **For thine's the power, the kingdom, glory evermore.**

NINTH CHILD. **Amen!**

Glory be to the Father; and to the Son; and to the Holy Ghost;
As it was in the beginning, is now and ever shall be,
World without end, Amen! Amen!

A PRAYER SERVICE.

FOR JUNIOR ENDEAVOR, OR EPWORTH LEAGUE MEETINGS; Or, it may be used in brief Supplemental Lessons in the Primary or Intermediate Departments; or as part of the opening exercises.

A PRAYER HYMN. *By E. M. Rawlings.*

TUNE. *Page 76.*

Our Father in heaven,
  All praise to thy name;
We bless thee, Lord Jesus,
  Whence all blessing came.
Keep us in thy presence,
  That others may see,
In our daily living,
  An image of thee.

And keep us from falling,
  Dear Father, we pray.
That so we may please thee,
  Our Saviour, each day.
Put in us thy Spirit;
  With his heavenly sword
We'll vanquish all evil,
  And honor our Lord.

1. Our Father who art in heaven, hallowed be Thy name. Thy kingdom come, Thy will be done on earth, as it is in heaven.

2. Give us this day our dai-ly bread, And forgive us our trespasses, as we forgive them that trespass a-gainst us.

3. And lead us not into temptation, but deliver us from evil: For Thine is the kingdom, and the power, and the glory, for ever and ever, A-men.

TEACHER. What is prayer?

SCH. Prayer is asking God for what we wish from the heart, and thanking him for what he has done for us.

TEACHER. To whom do we pray?

SCH. To God, our Father in heaven.

When are some of the times the Bible says we should pray?

SCH. Evening, and morning, and at noon, will I pray, and cry aloud. (Ps. 55:17.)

HYMN.

Ere you left your room this morning,
    Did you think to pray?
In the name of Christ, our Saviour,
    Did you plead his loving favor
As your shield to-day?

Or—

I will pray, I will pray,
    Night and morning every day;
Fold my hands and lift my eyes
    To my Jesus in the skies;
I will pray, I will pray,
    "Jesus, wash my guilt away;
Make my spirit pure within,
    Keep my soul from every sin."

A MORNING PRAYER.

Father, we thank thee for the night,
And for the pleasant morning light;
For rest and food and pleasant care,
And all that makes the day so fair.

Help us to do the things we should,
To be to others kind and good,
In all our work and all our play,
To love thee better every day.

TEACHER. Has Jesus promised to hear prayer?

SCH. Jesus said: "Ask and ye shall receive."

TEACHER. What should we do before we pray?

SCHOOL.

Before my words of prayer are said,
I'll close my eyes and bow my head,
I'll try to think to whom I pray,
And try to mean the words I say.

TEACHER. Why should we close eyes, bow heads, and fold hands?

SCHOOL.

We fold our hands that we may be
From all our work and play set free;
We bow our heads as we draw near
The King of kings, our Father dear;
We close our eyes that we may see
Nothing to take our thoughts from thee.

PRAYER.

CHANT. *Lord's Prayer* as above.

Dear Saviour, at thy throne we bow,
Oh, come and meet us now!
Let thy blessing, Lord, we pray,
Rest upon our class to-day

While we learn from out thy Word;
Oh, grant thy Spirit, Lord!
Help us each and every one.
This we ask for Christ, thy Son. AMEN.

Arranged by M. E. Reger.

COMMANDMENTS SERVICE.

This may be taught, one Commandment at a time, in five minute Supplemental or Preliminary lessons.

TEACHER. How many Commandments are there?

SCH. Ten.

TEACHER. Who gave them to us?

SCH. God.

TEACHER. How were they sent?

SCH. Through Moses.

TEACHER. On what were they written?

SCH. Two tables of stone.

TEACHER. How were they written?

SCH. **By the finger of God.**

TEACHER. Which Commandments were written on the first table?

SCH. **The first four Commandments, which tell us our duty to God.**

TEACHER. Which were written on the second table?

SCH. **The last six Commandments, which tell our duty to other people.**

MOTION EXERCISE.

Let us make our two little hands,[1] help us remember the Lord's Commands.
1, 2, 3, 4, 5,[2] 6, 7, 8, 9, 10, written on stone by God[3] for men.[14]
1. One God,[3] we have and one alone.
2. Then bow[4] not down to wood or stone.
3. Take not the name of God[3] in vain, nor soil our lips[5] with words profane.
4. The Sabbath day to God[3] belongs, we'll read[6] his Word and sing his songs.
5. Honor thy parents and obey, heeding[7] with care each word they say.
6. Thou shalt not kill, in thought or deed, anger[8] of murder sows the seed.
7. Both lips[5] and thoughts[9] must be kept clean; by God[3] our inmost heart[9] is seen.
8. "Thou shalt not steal,"[10] his eighth[11] command; watch well the acts of this small hand.[12]

9. Lie[5] not nor act what is untrue; tale-bearing is forbidden too.
10. "Thou shalt not covet,"[13] ends the Ten[1] Commandments given by God[3] to men.[14]

[1] Twinkle fingers on both hands. [2] Count on the fingers. [3] Point upwards. [4] Bow the knees slightly. [5] Finger on lips. [6] Hold hands like a book. [7] Point forefinger warningly. [8] Scowl. [9] Hand on heart. [10] Closed hands. [11] Hold up eight fingers. [12] Hold up hand. [13] Shake heads. [14] Drop hands to side.

THE FIRST COMMANDMENT.

HYMN. *(Little Pilgrim Songs.)*

Father, lead thy little children
Very early to thy throne;
We will have no gods before thee;
Thou art God, and thou alone.

Though the heathen bow to idols
They have made of wood and stone,
We have Christian friends to tell us.
Thou art God, and thou alone.

CHORUS.

Lead, oh, lead thy little children
Very early to thy throne;
We will have no gods before thee.
Thou art God, and thou alone.

TEACHER. What is the First Commandment?

SCH. **The First Commandment is: Thou shalt have no other gods before me.**

Lord, have mer-cy up-on us, and in-cline our hearts to keep this law.

TEACHER. What does the First Commandment forbid?

SCH. **The First Commandment forbids us to care for anything whatever more than we care for God.**

TEACHER. What command of Jesus shows the only true way to keep the First Commandment?

SCH. **Thou shalt love the Lord thy God with all thy heart.**

TEACHER. What is the Second Commandment?

SCH. **The Second Commandment is: Thou shalt not make unto thee any graven image, or likeness of any thing that is in heaven above, or that is in the earth beneath, or that is in the water under the earth:**
Thou shalt not bow down thyself to them, nor serve them: for I the Lord thy God am a jealous God, visiting the iniquity of the fathers

upon the children unto the third and fourth generation of them that hate me;
And shewing mercy unto thousands of them that love me, and keep my commandments.

TEACHER. What does the Second Commandment forbid?

SCH. **The Second Commandment forbids the use of images or pictures in our worship.**

TEACHER. What does it point out?

SCH. **The true way to worship.**

TEACHER. What does Jesus say of the true way to worship?

SCH. **God is a spirit, and they that worship him, must worship him in spirit and in truth.**

TEACHER. What is the Third Commandment?

SCH. **The Third Commandment is: Thou shalt not take the name of the Lord thy God in vain: for the Lord will not hold him guiltless that taketh his name in vain.**

TEACHER. What does the Third Commandment teach us?

SCH. How we ought to speak about God.

TEACHER. In what three ways is God's name taken in vain?

SCH. We take God's name in vain when we use it lightly without thinking; when we speak what is not true in connection with it; when we swear.

TEACHER. What did Jesus teach us to pray?

SCH. Hallowed be thy name.

HYMN.

Hush, little Christian child,
  Speak not that holy name!
Not in thy passion wild!
  Not in thy sportive game!
For the great Lord of all
  Heareth each word we say;
He will remember it
  At the great judgment day.

Honor God's holy name;
  Speak it with thought and care;
Sing it to solemn hymns;
  Breathe it in humble prayer;
But not with sudden call,
  In thy light joy or pain.
God will hold *guilty* all
  Who take his name in vain.

TEACHER. What is the Fourth Commandment?

SCH. The Fourth Commandment is: Remember the Sabbath day, to keep it holy. Six days shalt thou labour, and do all thy work:
But the seventh day is the Sabbath of the Lord thy God: in it thou shalt not do any work, thou, nor thy son, nor thy daughter, thy manservant, nor thy maidservant, nor thy cattle, nor thy stranger that is within thy gates:
For in six days the Lord made heaven and earth, the sea, and all that in them is, and rested the seventh day: wherefore the Lord blessed the Sabbath day, and hallowed it.

TEACHER. What does the Fourth Commandment forbid?

SCH. The Fourth Commandment forbids playing, learning weekday lessons, or doing weekday work.

TEACHER. How can we keep the Sabbath holy?

SCH. We should spend it in worshiping God, and in thinking and learning about him, and doing his work.

HYMN.

We 'll think not of work, nor of play,
  Nor talk of our meat or our drink;
But find all our pleasure to-day
  In thoughts *He* would have us to think.
We 'll talk of his works and his ways;
  We 'll speak of the marks of his love;
And learn the first notes of that praise
  We would sing with the ransomed above.

Thus best shall we hallow the day
That tells us that Jesus arose;
We 'll welcome its earliest ray,
  And keep it in peace till its close.
And then, when these Sabbaths are o'er,
  We 'll hope, at the last, to ascend
Where sin shall disturb us no more,
  The Sabbath of God have no end.

TEACHER. What is the Fifth Commandment?

SCH. The Fifth Commandment is: Honour thy father and thy mother: that thy days may be long upon the land which the Lord thy God giveth thee.

TEACHER. What is it to honor father and mother?

SCH. To respect, love, and obey them.

TEACHER. What does Paul say of this Commandment?

SCH. Honour thy father and mother, which is the first commandment with promise.

TEACHER. What reasons does Paul give for obedience to parents?

SCH. Children, obey your parents in all things, for this is well pleasing to the Lord.

TEACHER. Does this mean even if they should ask us to do wrong?

SCH. Children, obey your parents IN THE LORD, which means in all right things.

If thus earthly parents regard us with love,
  Oh! what shall we say of our Father above?
Lord, make us thy children, in spirit, that we
  May be always just what thou wouldst have
    us to be.

TEACHER. What is the Sixth Commandment?

SCH. The Sixth Commandment is: Thou shalt not kill.

TEACHER. What does the Sixth Commandment forbid?

SCH. The Sixth Commandment forbids injury to the lives of others; and injury to our own lives.

TEACHER. What does the apostle John tell us?

SCH. He that hateth his brother is a murderer.

There 's many a deed of murder done
  Where blood has ne'er been spilt;
For angry thoughts and words are one
  With deeds of crimson guilt.

Yes! in our hearts we often kill,
  And think the deed unknown;
Forgetting that each secret thought
  Is spoken at thy throne.

TEACHER. What is the Seventh Commandment?

SCH. The Seventh Commandment is: Thou shalt not commit adultery.

TEACHER. What does the Seventh Commandment forbid?

SCH. **The Seventh Commandment forbids all impure words and thoughts.**

> A heart in every thought renewed,
>   And full of love divine;
> Perfect and right and pure and good,
>   A copy, Lord, of thine.

TEACHER. What is the Eighth Commandment?

SCH. **The Eighth Commandment is: Thou shalt not steal.**

TEACHER. What does the Eighth Commandment forbid?

SCH. **The Eighth Commandment forbids our taking the smallest thing which belongs to another.**

TEACHER. What is the Ninth Commandment?

SCH. **The Ninth Commandment is: Thou shalt not bear false witness against thy neighbour.**

TEACHER. What does the Ninth Commandment forbid?

SCH. **The Ninth Commandment forbids all lying, deceiving, and slandering.**

TEACHER. What Bible prayer will help us to keep this commandment?

SCH. **Set a watch, O Lord, before my mouth; keep thou the door of my lips.**

TEACHER. What is the Tenth Commandment?

SCH. **The Tenth Commandment is: Thou shalt not covet thy neighbour's house, thou shalt not covet thy neighbour's wife, nor his manservant, nor his maidservant, nor his ox, nor his ass, nor any thing that is thy neighbour's.**

TEACHER. What does the Tenth Commandment forbid us to do?

SCH. **To wish for anything that belongs to another.**

> Is there, then, naught beneath, above,
>   That I may covet to possess?
> Yes; there's the Saviour's boundless love,
>   With which he waits my soul to bless.
>
> To me this treasure, Lord, impart;
>   Thy pardoning grace, oh! let me prove;
> Write thou thy laws upon my heart,
>   And make me covet all thy love.

Lord, have mercy up-on us, and write all these Thy laws in our hearts, we be-seech Thee.

TEACHER. What did Jesus call the First and Great Commandment?

SCH. **Thou shalt love the Lord thy God with all thy heart, and with all thy soul, and with all thy mind.**

TEACHER. What did he say was the Second, and like unto it?

SCH. **Thou shalt love thy neighbour as thyself.**

TEACHER. What New Commandment did Jesus give?

SCH. **Love one another.**

HYMN. TUNE: *Jesus loves me.*

> Jesus, help me day by day,
> All these precepts to obey;
> And the two thou gavest me:
> Love thy neighbor and love me.
>
> Dear Jesus, help me,
> Dear Jesus, help me,
> Dear Jesus, help me,
> Oh! help me to obey.

THE COMMANDMENTS IN VERSE.

> One God I must worship supreme,
>   And ne'er before images bow;

> I must not speak light of his name,
>   But pay to him every vow.
>
> I'm bound to remember with care
>   The Sabbath, so hallowed and pure;
> To honor my parents so dear,
>   That my life may the longer endure.
>
> I never must steal, or consent
>   To what is impure or untrue;
> I must not indulge discontent,
>   Nor covet my neighbor his due.
>
> Now help me, O Father in heaven,
>   To keep these commandments with zeal,
> In the strength that through Jesus is given,
>   To those who are doing thy will.

1. I am your God. Have none but me.
2. Before no likeness bow thy knee.
3. Breathe not God's name in rage or play.
4. Keep holy all the Sabbath day.
5. Honor your parents. Do their will.
6. Keep down your temper. Do not kill.
7. Let impure words and ways alone.
8. Take nothing that is not your own.
9. Speak truth. Talk not against your brothers,
10. Nor wish for what belongs to others.

M. G. K.

THE WAY OF SALVATION,

With Scripture Answers.

TEACHER. What have all men done?

SCHOLAR. All have sinned, and come short of the glory of God.

TEACHER. What is sin?

SCH. Sin is the transgression of the law.

TEACHER. Then are you, too, a sinner?

SCH. If we say we have no sin, we deceive ourselves, and the truth is not in us.

TUNE: *Jesus loves me.*

Jesus, Saviour, pity me,
Hear me when I cry to thee;
I've a very wicked heart,
Full of sin in every part.
    Dear Jesus, hear me!
    Oh! listen to my prayer.

TEACHER. What is the punishment for sin?

SCH. The soul that sinneth, it shall die.

TEACHER. Is that a light thing?

SCH. It is a fearful thing to fall into the hands of the living God.

TEACHER. Who fixed the punishment?

SCH. The great God, who formed all things.

TEACHER. Is there any possibility of your being overlooked?

SCH. We shall all stand before the judgment seat of Christ.

TEACHER. Who alone can make a way of escape?

SCH. I, even I, am the Lord; and beside me there is no Saviour.

Now I come to thee for aid,
All my hope on thee is stayed;
Thou hast bled and died for me,
I will give myself to thee.
    CHO. — Dear Jesus, hear me.

TEACHER. Is there no other way?

SCH. Neither is there salvation in any other; for there is none other name under heaven, given among men, whereby we must be saved.

TEACHER. What have we to do in order to be saved?

SCH. Repent ye, therefore, and be converted, that your sins may be blotted out.

C. M.

Repentance is to leave
    The sins we loved before,
And show that we in earnest grieve,
    By doing so no more.

TEACHER. What else must we do?

SCH. Believe on the Lord Jesus Christ, and thou shalt be saved.

TEACHER. What then becomes of our sins?

SCH. The blood of Jesus Christ, his Son, cleanseth us from all sin.

C. M.

There is a fountain filled with blood,
    Drawn from Immanuel's veins,
And sinners plunged beneath that flood,
    Lose all their guilty stains.

TEACHER. What is this salvation?

SCH. That whosoever believeth in him, should not perish, but have eternal life.

TEACHER. Will Jesus save all who come to him?

SCH. Him that cometh to me, I will in no wise cast out.

If I come to Jesus,
    He will make me glad;
He will give me pleasure,
    When my heart is sad.

If I come to Jesus,
    Happy shall I be:
He is gently calling
    Little ones like me.

TEACHER. Will he take even the worst sinner?

SCH. The Son of man is come to seek and to save that which is lost.

TEACHER. When is the right time to come to be saved?

SCH. Behold, now is the accepted time; behold, now is the day of salvation.

TEACHER. Suppose we neglect to attend to it?

SCH. How shall we escape if we neglect so great salvation?

TEACHER. What does Jesus say of some of us?

SCH. Ye will not come unto me, that ye might have life.

I lay my sins on Jesus,
    The spotless Lamb of God;
Who bears them all, and frees us
    From the accursed load.
I bring my guilt to Jesus,
    To wash my crimson stains
White, in his blood most precious,
    Till not a spot remains.

M. G. K.

JESUS AND THE CHILDREN.

GOOD NEWS FOR LITTLE CHILDREN.
Songs for Little Folks.   Page 66.

Good news for little children,
  Whoever they may be;
To them the loving Saviour
  Has said, " Come unto me."

CHORUS. — *To be chanted.*

Suffer little children to come unto me, and forbid them not;
For of such is the kingdom of heaven.

However poor and needy,
  However weak and small,
The boundless love of Jesus
  Encircles one and all.

CHO. — Suffer little children, etc.

None are to young to love him;
  None are too young to know
The name of h'm who saves them
  From endless death and woe.

CHO. — Suffer little children, etc.

TEACHER. Who were brought unto Jesus?

SCHOLAR. Little children.

TEACHER. Why were they brought to him?

SCH. That he should put his hands on
them, and pray.

TEACHER. What did his disciples do?

SCH. Rebuked those that brought them.

TEACHER. When Jesus saw it, how did he feel?

SCH. He was much displeased.

TEACHER. What did he say unto them?

SCH. Suffer little children, and forbid them
not, to come unto me; for of such is the kingdom of heaven.

TEACHER. What did Jesus then do to the
children?

SCH. He took them up in his arms, put his
hands upon them, and blessed them.

HYMN. — *Tune, p. 52.*

I think, when I read that sweet story of old,
  When Jesus was here among men,
How he called little children as lambs to his fold,
  I should like to have been with him then.

I wish that his hands had been placed on my
    head,
  That his arms had been thrown around me,
And that I might have seen his kind look when
    he said,
  " Let the little ones come unto me."

Yet still to his footstool in prayer I may go,
  And ask for a share in his love;
And if I thus earnestly seek him below,
  I shall see him and hear him above —

In that beautiful place he has gone to prepare,
  For all who are washed and forgiven;
And many dear children are gathering there:
  " For of such is the kingdom of heaven."

TEACHER. How must children, and all others,
be saved?

SCH. Except ye be converted, and become
as little children, ye shall not enter into the
kingdom of heaven.

TEACHER. What is the children's promise?

SCH. They that seek me early shall find me.

TEACHER. For what did Jesus thank his
Father?

SCH. That he had shown the way to heaven
to the children.

TEACHER. Where did the children praise
Jesus?

SCH. In the Temple.

TEACHER. What did they say?

SCH. Hosanna to the Son of David.

TEACHER. How can children best praise
Jesus?

SCH. By doing the things that please him.

SONG. *The Saviour's Call.* Page 85.

RECITATION.

JESUS AND THE CHILDREN.

(*For four little girls.*)

I know just the sweetest story
  That anyone ever heard,
How Jesus our own dear Saviour
  Said such a beautiful word.
And this is how it all happened
  (I can say every word by heart) :
They brought unto him young children —
  The Twelve said they must depart;
But Jesus, who sees and hears all things,
  Was displeased with these, his twelve friends,
And said (I beg you listen,
  For my hope on these words depends) : —

" Suffer the little children to come unto me,
and forbid them not; for of such is the kingdom of heaven."

I know one almost as pretty,
  And I will tell it to you.
One day the Twelve were disputing
  (As even they sometimes would do)
About who should be the greatest,
  And would not be reconciled.
Then Jesus, their Lord and Master,
  Taking a dear little child,
Set him amidst the disciples,
  With manner so gentle and sweet,
Then lifting him into his arms, said
  The words which now I repeat :—

" Verily I say unto you, Except ye be converted, and become as little children, ye shall
not enter into the kingdom of heaven."

It surely should make us happy
  That such things as these should be,
That the Lord, the King of Glory,
  Loves little ones such as we.

But you've not told all the story
  Of the day when the little child
  Taught the disciples this lesson —
    They must be humble and mild.
I am so glad I can tell you
  The very words he said,
  Lest some else should despise us
    When we went to him to be led : —
**"And whoso receiveth one such little child
in my name, receiveth me."**

No matter when little children
  Unto the dear Saviour came,
  He always gave them a blessing;
    And now it is just the same.
But I want you all to listen,
  While I my story repeat,
  Of when they cut off green branches,
    And cast them down at his feet,
Singing the while glad hosannas
  To Christ, their dear Lord and King;
  Then still again in the Temple,
    Loudly their praises did ring.
Some people cried out in their anger —
  " Hearest thou what those children say?"
  This is the beautiful answer
    Jesus made to them that day : —
**"Yea, have ye never read, Out of the
mouths of babes and sucklings thou hast per-
fected praise?"**

SONG. *He cares for me.* Page 70.

TEACHER. Are there any children who have
not heard of Jesus?

SCH. **There are many little children who
have never heard of his love and tenderness
or his Holy Word.**

Who are these children who have not heard
of Jesus?

    There are children, little children,
      In the lands beyond the sea,
    Who have never heard the tidings —
      " Let the children come to me."

    Heathen mothers bring their babies
      To the idol temples high,
    Clasp the tiny hands in worship,
      Prostrate both before them lie.

What does Jesus say to you about these little
brothers and sisters of yours?

FIRST CHILD.

    " If you love me," said the Master,
      " I ask of you a sign :
    Gather the little children;
      Go find these lambs of mine.

    To save their souls from dying,
      My life I've freely given;
    Yours be the task to lead them
      Up to my own bright heaven."

SECOND CHILD.

    What can the little children do
      For those that are lost in sin?
    How can they enter the " open gates"
      To carry the glad news in?

THIRD CHILD.

    Our little feet are too small to march
      In step with the mighty throng;
    But is there no work we can do for the King?
      For our love is true and strong.

ALL.

To every one he has given a part,
  And this is the children's share :
To willingly give of their own to the Lord,
  And send it forth with a prayer.

OFFERING. Taken by children.
  What more can children do to make the world
bright?

For four children.

Oh, what can little children do to make the great
  world glad?
For pain and sin are everywhere, and many a life
  is sad !
Our hearts must bloom with charity whenever
  sorrow lowers;
For how could summer days be sweet without
  the little flowers?

Oh, what can little children do to make the dark
  world bright?
For many a soul in shadow sits and longs to see
  the light.
Oh, we must lift our lamps of love, and let them
  gleam afar;
For how should night be beautiful without each
  little star?

Oh, what can little children do to bring some
  comfort sweet
For weary roads where men must climb with
  toiling, wayworn feet?
Our lives must ripple clear and fresh, that thirsty
  souls may sing;
Could robin pipe so merrily without the little
  spring?

All this may little children do, the saddened
  world to bless :
For God sends forth all loving souls to deeds of
  tenderness,
That this poor earth may bloom and sing like his
  dear home above;
But all the work would fail and cease without
  the children's love.

THE CHILDREN'S CORONATION.

TUNE: *Coronation.*

Hosanna be the children's song,
  To Christ the children's King.
His praise to whom our souls belong
  Let all the children sing.

From little ones to Jesus brought
  Hosanna now be heard,
Let little infants now be taught
  To lisp that loving word.

Hosanna, then, our song shall be,
  Hosanna to our King.
This is the Children's jubilee,
  Let all the children sing.

THE GOOD SHEPHERD.

A HYMN PRAYER.
8s, 7s, and 4s.

Saviour, like a shepherd lead us,
Much we need thy tend'rest care;
In thy pleasant pastures feed us,
For our use thy folds prepare.
Blessed Jesus,
Thou hast bought us, thine we are.

We are thine, do thou befriend us,
Be the Guardian of our way;
Keep thy flock, from sin defend us,
Seek us when we go astray.
Blessed Jesus
Hear, oh, hear us when we pray!

THE TWENTY-THIRD PSALM.

1. The Lord is my shepherd; I shall not want.
2. He maketh me to lie down in green pastures: he leadeth me beside the still waters.
3. He restoreth my soul: he leadeth me in the paths of righteousness for his name's sake.
4. Yea, though I walk through the valley of the shadow of death, I will fear no evil: for thou art with me; thy rod and thy staff they comfort me.
5. Thou preparest a table before me in the presence of mine enemies: thou anointest my head with oil; my cup runneth over.
6. Surely goodness and mercy shall follow me all the days of my life: and I will dwell in the house of the Lord for ever.

RECITATION. For twelve children. The answering texts may be given by the whole class if desired.

FIRST.

Little lambs of the flock
Our teachers do call us;
Then who is our Shepherd,
Ever watching
Lest harm should befall us?

Jesus said, "I am the good shepherd." (John 10:11.)

SECOND.

But is he not a Shepherd
To watch and tend the sheep,
While tender little lambs,
Seeming useless,
No time he has to keep?

He shall gather the lambs with his arm, and carry them in his bosom. (Isa. 40:11.)

THIRD.

Carry them in his bosom?
Gather them in his arm?
There may I sweetly slumber,
Peaceful, resting
Secure from every harm?

I will both lay me down in peace, and sleep: for thou, Lord, only makest me dwell in safety. (Ps. 4:8.)

FOURTH.

But when this kind Shepherd
Himself doth need to sleep,
Then who will watch o'er me,
Kindly caring
Such little ones to keep?

He that keepeth thee will not slumber. Behold, he that keepeth Israel shall neither slumber nor sleep. (Ps. 121:3, 4.)

FIFTH.

Suppose that I should wander,
Far from the path should stray,
Would the Shepherd miss me?
Would he seek me,
And show me the right way?

Behold I, even I, will both search my sheep, and seek them out. As a shepherd seeketh out his flock in the day that he is among his sheep that are scattered; so will I seek out my sheep, and will deliver them out of all places where they have been scattered in the cloudy and dark day. (Ezek. 34:11, 12.)

SIXTH.

But I am very tiny,
And am not very strong;
And if I should be sick
Or broken down,
I could not follow long.

I will seek that which was lost, and bring again that which was driven away, and will bind up that which is broken, and will strengthen that which was sick. (Ezek. 34:16.)

SONG. TUNE: *I am so glad.* (Gospel Hymns, No. 23.)

The Lord is my Shepherd, and I am his lamb,
One of the smallest and frailest I am,
Yet by his bounty daily I'm fed,
In his green pastures tenderly led.

CHORUS.

He is my Shepherd, I am so glad,
For he loves me; for he loves me;
He is my Shepherd, I am so glad,
For he loves even me.

Kind is my Shepherd, and large is the fold
To which he calleth the young as the old,
Tenderly watching in waking and sleep,
Over us, evermore, guard he doth keep. — CHO.

Sometimes the way where he leadeth his sheep
Grows for my child-feet dark and too steep;
Then doth he lift me up close to his breast,
Bearing me upward to places of rest. — CHO.

When I had wandered away from his side,
Into the paths which the sinning have tried,
He, o'er each step of sin's rugged track,
Patiently, lovingly, guided me back. — CHO.

He hath green pastures — lying afar —
Needing no sunlight, needing no star.
There, from his presence, the lambs *never* stray;
Thither he leadeth me — nearer each day. — Cho.

But closer than meadows brightened by faith,
Lieth the valley of silence and death;
Seeing its shadows — yet fearless I am,
*For the Lord is my Shepherd, and I am his
    lamb!* —Cho.

SEVENTH.

Oh, what a dear, kind Shepherd!
    Would that I were not so small,
That I might surely hear him,
        Plainly hear him,
    If for me he should call.

My sheep hear my voice, and I know them.
(John 10:27.)

EIGHTH.

If he would only know me,
    When unto him I came,
How happy it would make me,
    If he should speak,
    And call me by name!

He calleth his own sheep by name. (John
10:3.)

NINTH.

How shall I know which road
Is the right way to go,
Unless some one goes before,
    A little way,
    That I the path may know?

**When he putteth forth his own sheep, he
goeth before them, and the sheep follow him:
for they know his voice.** (John 10:4.)

TENTH.

If any danger threatens
    Such a helpless little lamb,
Can I run right to Jesus?
        Will he protect
    And hold me by the hand?

**The good shepherd giveth his life for the
sheep.** (John 10:11.)

ELEVENTH.

Surely this gentle Shepherd
    Has nothing more to give,
When he laid down his life,
        His precious life,
    That his own lambs might live?

**I give unto them eternal life; and they
shall never perish.** (John 10:28.)

TWELFTH.

Oh, help us, tender Shepherd,
    To go where thou dost lead us,
To follow in thy footsteps;
    In pastures green, oh, feed us,
        Loving Saviour;
Help every little lamb
To live so very near thee,
That each on thy right hand
Among thy sheep may stand
        At the last day.
Oh, bear us, gentle Jesus,
    As in the days of old,
Take us, when our work is done,
    Home to the upper fold.

SINGING. TUNE: *Near the Cross.*

I was but a little lamb
    From the Saviour straying,
When I heard within my heart
    Some one softly saying:
" Follow me, follow me,
    I will safely guide thee
Through the stormy ways of life,
    Walking close beside thee."

Into danger I would go
    But for this protection;
I should miss of heaven, I know,
    But for this direction:
" Follow me, follow me,
    I will safely guide thee
Through the stormy ways of life,
    Walking close beside thee."

Never turning from that voice,
    Never disobeying,
Let me know that unto me
    Christ is always saying:
" Follow me, follow me,
    I will safely guide thee
Through the stormy ways of life,
    Walking close beside thee."

Early to his loving care
    Shall my heart be given,
For each step I take with him
    Brings me nearer heaven.
" Follow me, follow me,"
    Is the Saviour saying
Unto every little lamb
    Who from him is straying.

CLOSING PRAYER BY CLASS.

Jesus, tender Shepherd, hear me,
    Bless thy little lamb to-night;
Through the darkness be thou near me,
    Keep me safe till morning light.

M. G. K.

LESSONS ABOUT THE BIBLE.

TEACHER. What are the seven names for this book?

SCHOLAR. 1. Oracles — God's message to us.

    2. Word — God's message spoken.

    3. Scripture — God's message written.

    4. Bible — God's message written in a book.

    5. Canon — God's message the rule of our lives.

    6. Law — God's message a law for us.

    7. Testament — God's message his covenant with us.

TEACHER. How did God give his message?

SCH. Through thirty-six men who wrote what the Holy Spirit taught them.

TEACHER. When did these men write?

SCH. Through sixteen centuries, from 1500 B.C. to 100 A.D.

TEACHER. In what language did they write?

SCH. In Hebrew, Chaldee, and Greek.

TEACHER. How then can we understand what they wrote?

SCH. It was changed into English in 1611, by command of King James; and this has lately been revised by a committee of learned men.

BLACKBOARD OUTLINE.

— *Young Traveler's Leaflets.*

The Contents of the New Testament Books are taught in *Walks and Talks about Jesus*, published by Hunt & Eaton, New York.

A pamphlet of Lessons on the Books of the Bible, by Mr. I. P. Black, is published by the Presbyterian Board, Philadelphia.

THE BOOKS OF THE BIBLE.

The connecting verses might be recited by one child, or a group of children; the names of the books by the school.

> The Bible is a library of books inspired by God,
> They number sixty-six in all, and spread his truth abroad.
> Divided into Testaments, of these there are but two,
> Books thirty-nine are in the Old, twenty-seven in the New.

> Five *books of law* by Moses, called The Pentateuch; we'll learn
> Their names in proper order, as we say them each in turn.

GEN. EX. LEV. NUM. DEUT.

> Twelve *books of history* record
> The wondrous dealings of the Lord.

JOSHUA JUDGES RUTH I SAM. II SAM. I KINGS II KINGS I CHRON. II CHRON. EZRA NEH. ESTHER

> Five *books of poetry* come next
> In order, in the Sacred Text.

JOB PSALMS PROV. ECC. S OF SOL

> Then *greater prophets*, five, we see;
> Hard names, and we must careful be.

ISA. JER. LAM. EZEK. DAN.

> Twelve *lesser prophets* close the long, long list;
> The Books of the Old Testament: not one we've missed.

> Ho., Jo., Am., and Ob., Jo., Mi., Na.;
> Ha., Ze., Ha., Ze., Ma.

BOOKS OF THE NEW TESTAMENT.

Then, Jesus, blessed Saviour, came,
And four who loved him well
Wrote books that of his life and death
And resurrection, tell:
Matthew, Mark, Luke, and John;
We call them " Gospel" books,
And he who reads them, on the love
Of Christ our Saviour looks.

Acts is a history of the stirring time
Apostles taught, and lived the faith sublime.
"Acts of the Apostles."

Then came some precious letters, written
The Christian life upon;
By Paul and James and Peter,
Jude and John.

There are *twenty-one* letters in all,
Fourteen of which were written by Paul.

Nine of these were written to churches. These are Rom., 1 Cor., 2 Cor., Gal., Eph., Phil., Col., 1 Thess., 2 Thess.
Then four letters from Paul to dearly loved friends: 1 Tim., 2 Tim., Titus, Philemon.
Then *Hebrews*, written to Christian Jews.
Seven letters, written by *four* Apostles: one by James, two by Peter, three by John, and a little one by Jude.

The book of Revelation is the close of Bible story,
Oh, come to Jesus, and you'll know the riches of its glory.

E. E. HEWITT.

A SUNDAY-SCHOOL QUESTION.

The Sunday-school about to close,
A stranger in the pulpit rose.

He held the Bible up to view;
A question, boys and girls, for you:

"How many books, if all were told,
In the new Testament and Old?"

Of all that band
None raised a hand,
Or offered a suggestion;
Some were amused,
And some confused.
At such a simple question.

Alas! alas!
The Bible-class,
Though some were trained in college,
Abashed, ashamed,
When they were named,
Confessed their lack of knowledge.

The stranger said: "If you don't know,
An easy method I will show

By which their number you can find,
And keep it always in your mind;

In O-l-d you find just letters three,
In T-e-s-t-a-m-e-n-t just nine, you see.

Now place these figures side by side,
And let them there in peace abide,

Then, surely as the sun doth shine.
You'll find you have just thirty-nine.

N-e-w T-e-s-t-a-m-e-n-t — well, let us see:
Once more nine letters, once more three.

Your three by nine please multiply,
And twenty-seven meets your eye.

Add both the numbers you've obtained,
And the right answer you have gained;

By two nice figures you'll be told
How many books your Bibles hold.

Now just alike these figures are,
In truth they make a pretty pair.

If you subtract the Sabbath day
From one full week, then, strange to say,

Of these two figures you'll get one,
Put down the other and it's done."

WHAT THE SIXTY-SIX BOOKS TELL.

In Genesis the world was made;
  In Exodus the march is told;
Leviticus contains the law;
  In Numbers are the tribes enrolled.
In Deuteronomy again
  We're urged to keep God's law alone;
And these five books of Moses make
  The oldest writings that are known.

Brave Joshua to Canaan leads;
  In Judges oft the Jews rebel;
We read of David's name in Ruth
  And First and Second Samuel.
In first and Second Kings we read
  How bad the Hebrew state became,
In First and Second Chronicles
  Another history of the same.
In Ezra captive Jews return,
  And Nehemiah builds the wall;
Queen Esther saves her race from death,
  These books "historical" we call.

In Job we read of patient faith;
  The Psalms are David's songs of praise;
The Proverbs are to make us wise;
  Ecclesiastes next portrays
How fleeting earthly pleasures are:
  The Song of Solomon is all
About the love of Christ; and these
  Five books "poetical" we call.

Isaiah tells of Christ to come,
  While Jeremiah tells of woe,
And in his Lamentations mourns
  The Holy City's overthrow.
Ezekiel speaks of mysteries,
  And Daniel foretells kings of old;
Hosea calls men to repent;
  In Joel blessings are foretold.

Amos tells of wrath; and Edom
  Obadiah's sent to warn;
While Jonah shows that Christ should die,
  And Micah where he should be born.
In Nahum Nineveh is seen;
  In Habakkuk Chaldea's guilt;
In Zephaniah Judah's sins;
  In Haggai the temple built;
Zechariah speaks of Christ,
  And Malachi, of John, his sign;
The prophets number seventeen,
  And all the books are thirty-nine.

Matthew, Mark and Luke and John
  Tell what Christ did in every place;
Acts show what the apostles did,
  And Romans how we're saved by grace.
Corinthians instructs the church;
  Galatians shows us faith alone;
Ephesians true love, and in
  Philippians God's grace is shown.
Colossians tells us more of Christ,
  And Thessalonians of the end;
In Timothy and Titus both
  Are rules for pastors to attend.

Philemon Christian friendship shows;
  Then Hebrews clearly tells us how all
The Jewish law prefigured Christ;
  And these epistles are by Paul.
James shows that faith by works must live,
  And Peter urges steadfastness,
While John exhorts to Christian love,
  For those who have it God will bless.
Jude shows the end of evil men,
  And Revelation tells of heaven.
This ends the whole New Testament,
  And all the books are twenty-seven.

BEREAN BIBLE BAND.

Membership in this Band composed of members of the Primary or Junior department is secured by repeating before the school, without help, the names of the books of the Bible. *Bible Day*, once a month. Let a portion of the opening exercises be omitted and a Drill in the Books of the Bible be given.

TEACHER. What is the name of this Band?

SCHOOL. Berean Bible Band.

TEACHER. Why have we chosen this name?

SCH. Because the people of Berea were more noble than those of Thessalonica in that they searched the Scriptures daily.

TEACHER. From what book are all our lessons taken?

SCH. From God's blessed book the Bible.

TEACHER. If it is God's Word, how should we listen?

SCH. With our eyes, that we may see. With our ears, that we may hear. With our hearts, that we may do the things that we are told.

TEACHER. How can we listen with our eyes?

SCH. By reading God's Word

TEACHER. What Bible prayer is given to help us see with our eyes?

SCH. "**Open thou mine eyes, that I may behold wondrous things out of thy law.**"

TEACHER. How can we listen with our ears?

SCH. **By paying attention when God's Word is read to us.**

TEACHER. What Bible prayer will help us to understand the reading?

SCH. "**Speak, Lord, thy servant heareth.**"

TEACHER. How may we do with our hearts what we are taught in the Bible?

SCH. **By asking God to send his Holy Spirit to help us.**

TEACHER. What Bible prayers do we find for this need?

BOYS. **Incline our hearts to keep his law.**

GIRLS. **Incline my heart unto thy testimonies.**

TEACHER. What did the Psalmist say about God's word in the heart?

SCH. "**Thy word have I hid in mine heart, that I might not sin against thee.**"

TEACHER. What is the most important thing in the Bible?

SCH. **How to be saved.**

TEACHER. What is this truth, and where do we find it?

SCH. **In John 3:16.**—For God so loved the world that he gave his only begotten Son, that whosoever believeth in him should not perish but have everlasting life.

HYMN, *How Sweet is the Bible.* Page 52.

M. E. REGER.

BIBLE GEOGRAPHY.

Bible Geography, especially that of Palestine, should be taught in the Primary class, unless the children are transferred to the Intermediate department, at about eight years of age. In the latter, both Old and New Testament Geography should be thoroughly taught. In the Primary class the sand table should be used. In the Intermediate, the map should be drawn before the class on the blackboard.

Progressive lessons by the Editor of this book are in three sets of leaflets: 1. *Young Traveler's Class.* 2. *Walks and Talks with Jesus.* 3. *The Bible Story.* These consist of seven lessons each, at ten cents per set. Published by Hunt & Eaton, New York.

GUIDE TO MAP DRAWING.
WHERE TO PLACE THE CITIES AND MOUNTAINS.

A dotted line from the *north* of the Dead Sea to the coast; one third of the way on this line place Jerusalem. Another dotted line from the *south* of the Sea of Galilee to the coast; halfway along this line is Nazareth, where Jesus lived when a boy. Halfway along a straight line from Nazareth to Jerusalem is Shechem, or Sychar, where Jesus talked with a ——. On each side of Sychar are the twin mountains Ebal and Gerizim. Halfway between the top and the "thumb" of the Dead Sea draw a line through Jerusalem to the coast and you will find Joppa, where we landed. Go *south* from Joppa right along the seacoast, and halfway down place Gaza, where —— carried off the gates. In the "crook" in the coast line is Mt. Carmel, where Elijah ——. Halfway from Carmel to Joppa is Cesarea, where P—— was in prison two years. From Gaza, a line through Jerusalem to the river Jordan, and we have J——, whose walls fell down. Travel *south* from Jerusalem on a slightly circular line and we come first to Bethlehem, where ——, then to Hebron, where Abraham lived, and last to Beersheba, which is the most southern town in Palestine. Away up north on the east of the Jordan is Dan, farthest north of the cities; but still farther north towers snow-covered Mt. Hermon. Capernaum is on the northwest of the Sea of G——, and Bethany, where Jesus loved to go, just east of Jerusalem, on Mt. Olivet. East of the Sea is Mt. Nebo, where Moses died.

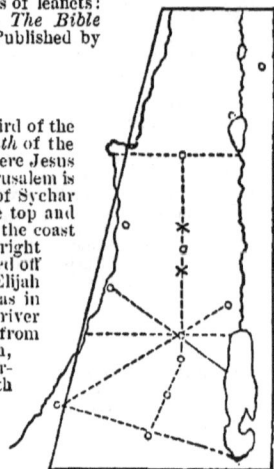

FOOTSTEPS IN THE HOLY LAND.

A child may point out the place named in one verse, then another the next place, and so on. Or, after the map has been taught, the child may *mark* each city.

SING, *There is a Holy Land called Palestine.* Page 65.

TEACHER. What is this country called?

SCHOOL. **Palestine.**

TEACHER. Why was it so called?

SCH. From the Philistines.

TEACHER. Who was one of the Philistines?

SCH. Goliath, the Giant.

TEACHER. What is the first Bible name for this land?

SCH. Canaan.

TEACHER. Why was it so called?

SCH. Because Noah's grandson, Canaan, lived there after the flood.

TEACHER. To whom was this land promised?

SCH. To Abraham.

TEACHER. Therefore what was it called?

SCH. The promised land.

TEACHER. What do *we* love to call it?

SCH. The Holy Land.

TEACHER. Why do we give it that name?

SCH. Because Jesus was born there, and it was there he did his wonderful works, and there he died for me.

SINGING, to tune *Who is He?* page 16, Songs for Little Folks, and in many other books.

> Christ in Palestine did stand,
> Making Canaan holy land.

TEACHER. Into how many parts was Canaan divided after the children of Israel went back?

SCHOOL. Into twelve parts.

TEACHER. Why were there that number?

SCH. That each one of the twelve tribes or families of the sons of Jacob might have a share.

TEACHER. Into how many parts was it divided in the time of Jesus?

SCH. Into three parts.

TEACHER. Name them.

SCH. Judea on the south, Samaria in the middle, Galilee in the north.

TEACHER. In which one of these was Jesus born?

SCH. In Judea, in the city of Bethlehem.

TEACHER. What is the meaning of the word Bethlehem?

SCH. The House of Bread.

TEACHER. Why was it fitting that Jesus should be born in a place with such a name?

SCH. Jesus is the Bread of Life.

TEACHER. Who went to see him?

SCH. Shepherds who were watching their flocks near the city.

SING.

> As he lay in *Bethlehem's* stall,
> At his feet the shepherds fall.

TEACHER. Where did Jesus live when he was a boy?

SCH. In Nazareth.

TEACHER. Where is Nazareth?

SCH. In Galilee.

TEACHER. What is the Fifth Commandment?

SCH. "Honour thy father and thy mother, that thy days may be long upon the land which the Lord thy God giveth thee."

TEACHER. Did Jesus keep this commandment?

SCH. He was obedient unto his parents.

SING.

> This good Son in *Nazareth* stayed,
> And his parents he obeyed.

TEACHER. What journey did Jesus take when he was a boy?

SCH. From Nazareth to Jerusalem.

TEACHER. How far was that?

SCH. About seventy miles.

TEACHER. In which of the divisions of Palestine was Jerusalem?

SCH. In Judea.

TEACHER. Why did he go there?

SCH. He went with his parents to keep the Passover.

TEACHER. How old was he at this time?

SCH. Twelve years old.

TEACHER. When they returned what did Jesus do?

SCH. The child Jesus tarried behind in Jerusalem.

TEACHER. What did his parents find him doing?

SCH. They found him in the temple, sitting in the midst of the doctors, both hearing them and asking them questions.

SING.

> This wise boy, whom parents sought,
> In *Jerusalem's* temple taught.

TEACHER. Where was Jesus baptized?

SCH. In the river Jordan.

TEACHER. In what part of it?

SCH. Near Bethabara, about twenty miles from Jerusalem.

TEACHER. What can you tell us of this river?

SCH. It rises in the north, near Mount Hermon, runs right through the Sea of Galilee, and empties into the Dead Sea. It is very crooked, and rushes along very rapidly.

SING.

> "Suffer it," the Saviour said,
> And to *Jordan's* stream was led.

TEACHER. Where did Jesus work his first miracle?

SCH. At Cana of Galilee, about seven miles north of Nazareth.

TEACHER. What was this miracle?

SCH. He turned water into wine at a wedding.

TEACHER. What words that his mother said to the servants at that time would it be well for us to keep in mind?

SCH. "Whatsoever he saith unto you, do it."

SING.
> There in *Cana of Galilee*,
> Water into wine turned he.

TEACHER. Where was Jacob's well?

SCH. In Samaria.

TEACHER. Near to what city?

SCH. Sychar, which was formerly called Shechem.

TEACHER. Why was it called Jacob's Well?

SCH. It was a parcel of ground which Jacob gave his son Joseph.

TEACHER. What did Jesus do there?

SCH. Taught a woman about the water of life.

SING.
> Of living water he did tell
> Samaria's woman at the well.

TEACHER. What sea is in the northern part of the Holy Land?

SCH. The Sea of Galilee.

TEACHER. By what other names was it called?

SCH. Lake Tiberias and Lake Gennesaret.

TEACHER. How did Jesus go over it once?

SCH. He walked on the water.

TEACHER. Where was he going?

SCH. To Capernaum.

TEACHER. Where is Capernaum?

SCH. On the shore of the lake, about twenty miles from Nazareth.

TEACHER. What did Jesus do at Capernaum?

SCH. He healed the son of a nobleman.

SING.
> Towards *Capernaum*, who is he
> Walked the *Sea of Galilee?*

TEACHER. Here is a little town of only four letters. What is it?

SCH. Nain.

TEACHER. In which of the three divisions is Nain?

SCH. In Galilee.

TEACHER. What wonder did Jesus work near there?

SCH. He raised a dead man to life.

TEACHER. What do you know of this young man?

SCH. He was the only son of his mother, and she was a widow.

SING.
> Christ the widow's son, of *Nain*,
> Raised from death to life again.

TEACHER. There was a little town only two miles from Jerusalem, where Jesus loved to go. What was it?

SCH. Bethany.

TEACHER. Who lived in Bethany?

SCH. The two sisters, Martha and Mary, and their brother Lazarus.

TEACHER. What miracle did Jesus do in Bethany?

SCH. He raised Lazarus to life.

SING.
> Christ in *Bethany* stands and weeps
> O'er the grave where Lazarus sleeps.

TEACHER. What garden lay in a valley outside of the walls of Jerusalem?

SCH. Gethsemane.

TEACHER. When did Jesus go there?

SCH. On Thursday, the night before he died.

TEACHER. What happened to him there?

SCH. Being in great agony, he prayed, "Father, if it be possible, let this cup pass from me."

TEACHER. Who found him in the Garden of Gethsemane?

SCH. Judas, who betrayed him.

SING.
> In *Gethsemane* see him now,
> On the ground at midnight bow.

TEACHER. How did Jesus die?

SCH. He was crucified.

TEACHER. Why did he die?

SCH. For our sins, that we might be saved.

TEACHER. Where was he crucified?

SCH. On a hill called Calvary.

TEACHER. By what other name was it called?

SCH. The Hebrew word Golgotha, which means the place of a skull.

SING.
> On the cross, on *Calvary's* side,
> Christ our Lord was crucified.

TEACHER. How long did he lie in the grave?

SCH. Three days.

TEACHER. How long did he stay on earth?

SCH. Forty days.

TEACHER. What happened then?

SCH. He ascended into heaven.

TEACHER. From what place?

SCH. From the mount which is called Olivet.

SING.
> See him now, on *Olivet's* height,
> Clouds receive him out of sight.

CHORUS, to be sung only after the last couplet:

> Jesus, who on earth did dwell,
> Son of God and man as well,
> Take us gently by the hand —
> Lead us to the better land.

THE SONG OF THE HOLY LAND, page 66, may be sung between each part, or used at the close.

M. G. K

LITTLE CHRISTIANS.

TEACHER. Can little children be Christians?

BOYS. Yes. Jesus said, "Suffer the little children to come unto me, and forbid them not: for of such is the Kingdom of God."

GIRLS. Jesus said, "Verily I say unto you, Except ye be converted and become as little children, ye shall not enter into the Kingdom of Heaven."

TEACHER. Who are little Christians?

SCHOOL. Little Christians are children who come to the Lord Jesus, that he may take away their sins with his precious blood; and who love and try to please him.

SING, *Trust and Obey* (one verse).

TEACHER. Is it hard to come to Jesus?

SCH. No: he is always near; "ready to forgive," "mighty to save."

TEACHER. How can we please the Lord Jesus?

SCH. Jesus says: "If ye love me, keep my commandments."

TEACHER. Can we do this in our own strength?

SCH. No; we cannot keep God's commandments without his help.

TEACHER. When must we ask his help?

SCH. Every night and morning, and whenever tempted to do wrong.

TEACHER. Will he surely help us, when we truly ask?

SCH. "Ask, and ye shall receive."

SING, *Ask the Saviour to help you.*

TEACHER. Can little children live with Jesus in Heaven, if they do not grow like him here?

SCH. No. We must grow like Jesus if we would live with him in Heaven.

TEACHER. How can we grow like Jesus?

BOYS. We must "watch and pray."

GIRLS. "Search the Scriptures."

ALL. "Looking unto Jesus," who is "able to keep us from falling."

TEACHER. What "Golden Rule" does Jesus give?

SCH "Whatsoever ye would that men should do to you do ye even so to them."

Whether I am at home, or school,
  Wherever I may be,
Lord, help me to obey this rule
  Which thou hast taught to me:
To do to others, as I would
  That they should do to me,
For this will make me kind and good,
  As thou would'st have me be.

(Recited as a prayer; bowed heads and clasped hands.)

TEACHER. Can even little Christians honor the Saviour?

GIRLS. "Even a child is known by his doings, whether his work be pure, and whether it be right."

BOYS. "He that is faithful in that which is least is faithful also in much."

TEACHER. What other sweet rules does the Bible give for daily life?

GIRLS. "Love one another."

BOYS. "Be not overcome with evil, but overcome evil with good."

SING, *Children, do you love each other?*

TEACHER. Which is the commandment with promise?

SCHOOL. The Fifth Commandment, which is: "Honour thy father and thy mother, that thy days may be long upon the land which the Lord thy God giveth thee."

TEACHER. Are we to obey our parents and teachers only when they see us?

SCH. No; at all times. "As servants of Christ, doing the will of God from the heart."

TEACHER. How must little Christians keep the Sabbath?

SCH. The Fourth Commandment says: "Remember the Sabbath day to keep it holy."

SING, *I'm always glad when Sunday comes.* (Infant Praises.)

TEACHER. How should we take "our daily bread"?

SCH. We should take "our daily bread" from our Father in Heaven, cheerfully, thankfully, asking his blessing.

SING, *God is great, and God is good.*

TEACHER. How can our lips honor Jesus?

BOYS. "Speaking the truth in love."

GIRLS. "The words of the pure are pleasant words."

SING, *Set a watch, O Lord.* (Infant Praises.)

TEACHER. What Bible verse covers our whole lives?

SCH. Whatsoever ye do, do all to the glory of God.

TEACHER. What sweet words will Jesus say hereafter, to those who love and serve him here?

SCH. "Come, ye blessed of my Father, inherit the kingdom prepared for you from the foundation of the world."

SING, *Around the throne of God in Heaven.*

E. E. HEWITT.

HOW WE REMEMBER OUR BIBLE VERSES.

A MOTION EXERCISE.

This may be used a verse or two at a time to quiet restlessness. Or on an Anniversary occasion ten children may take part; all repeat the verses with the appropriate movements, and a single voice the Scripture recitations.

This is the way a little child,
Remembers Bible verses,
Come, listen, all you grown-up folks,
While he these things rehearses.

The *heavens* are high the *earth* above,
This teaches us how great *God's* love.

For as the heaven is high above the earth, so great is his mercy toward them that fear him. (Ps. 103 : 11.)

Now to the *east*, and to the *west*,
I 'll point while I repeat my text.

As far as the east is from the west, so far hath he removed our transgressions from us. (Ps. 103 : 12.)

The *rain* comes down, also the *snow*
Waters the seed which *sowers* sow.

The rain cometh down and the snow from heaven and returneth not thither, but watereth the earth, and maketh it to bring forth and bud, that it may give seed to the sower, and bread to the eater. (Is. 55 : 10.)

One *narrow* way, one *broad and wide*;
Enter the *straight*, choose none beside.

Enter ye in at the strait gate; for wide is the gate, and broad is the way that leadeth to destruction, and many there be that go in thereat. (Matt. 7 : 13.)

This my *left* hand, this my *right*,
What verse should these help me recite?

Ponder the path of thy feet, and let all thy ways be established. Turn not to the right hand, nor to the left. (Prov. 4 : 26.)

Behind us now our arms we throw.
Behind him, Jesus bid Satan go.

Get thee behind me, Satan. (Mark 4 : 8.)

Jesus *gathers* the lambs with his *arm*,
There they are safe from every harm.

He shall feed his flock like a shepherd, he shall gather the lambs with his arm. (Is. 40 : 11.)

In his bosom carries them too;
I think that very sweet, don't you?

And carry them in his bosom. (Is. 40 : 11.)

As soon as they his lambs became,
On their *foreheads* he wrote his name.

And they shall see his face; and his name shall be in their foreheads. (Rev. 22 : 4.)

Right joyfully we *clap our hands*,
Jesus *shall* reign o'er all the lands.

Oh, clap your hands, all ye people; shout unto God with a voice of triumph. He is a great king over all the earth.

Yet once more we will rehearse,
How we remember each our verse.
See, this is *west*, and this is *east*:
The heavens are *high*, the earth is *least*.
The raindrops *pitter patter* so;
Thus *gently* falls the pure white snow.
Narrow or *wide*, which will you take?
Behind, the motion we now make.
These our *right* hands are, you see,
And these our *left*, we all agree.
This way we each our *arms will fold*,
As though we all, a lamb did hold.
Upon our *foreheads* which are here,
May Jesus write his name so dear.
And when again we *clap our hands*,
We hope that each friend understands
We only make these pretty signs
To keep in mind our Bible lines.

From the word *clap*, fourth line from last, all clap hands to a close; each shakes hands with neighbor, and all throw a kiss exactly together to the audience. The motions are so simple they seem to need no explanation.

M. G. K.

LITTLE HANDS.

A MOTION EXERCISE.

This also may be used a couplet at a time with the accompanying text when a change of position is needed; or it may be used by eleven children at an anniversary. Children arranged in a semicircle.

In Concert.
Two little hands, so white and fair;
Five little fingers, each has for its share;
Five have the *left* hand, five the *right*;
Ten this makes, so plain in your sight.
Hands that can work, hands that can play,

Quite useful little friends are they.
And now we 'll show you something new,
That children's hands can find to do,
Fold, little hands, till each in your turn
Help us our Bible texts to learn.

One steps out from the others and asks the questions; the rest reply in exact concert with suitable hand motions.

Hold up your *right hands*, one and all;
What do these right hands loudly call?

ALL; raising right hands. For I, the Lord thy God, will hold thy right hand, saying unto thee, Fear not, I will help thee. (Is. 41:13.)

11. *Left hands* raise high, it is their turn;
What verse have they for us to learn?

ALL; raising left hands. But when thou doest alms, let not thy left hand know what thy right hand doeth. (Matt. 6:3.)

2. *Right* hands and *left* together hold;
What sight do these help us behold?

ALL; separating both hands to the right and left. And he shall set the sheep on his right hand, but the goats on the left. (Matt. 25:33.)

10. Who in his *bosom hides* his hands,
And will not work or till the land?

ALL; with hands in bosom. A slothful man hideth his hand in his bosom, and will not so much as bring it to his mouth again. (Prov. 19:24.)

3. With *folded hands*, what does he say,
When the sun calls "Awake! 't is day"?

ALL; hands folded across bosom, heads sleeply nodding. Yet a little sleep, a little slumber, a little folding of the hands to sleep. (Prov. 6:10.)

9. What says the Bible do you know
Of *closed* hands, and *wide open* — so?

ALL; hands tightly closed, then held straight out wide open. Thou shalt not harden thine heart, nor shut thine hand from thy poor brother. But thou shalt open thine hand wide unto him. (Deut. 15:7, 8.)

4. What wall was raised, on *left and right,*
That showed to Israel their God's might?

ALL; arms outstretched on each side like a wall. The children of Israel went into the midst of the sea, upon the dry ground; and the waters were a wall unto them, on their right hand and on their left. (Ex. 14:22.)

8. Held in the *hollow* of God's hand,
The great sea cannot burst its band.

ALL; hands held together like a hollow scoop. Who hath measured the waters in the hollow of his hand. (Is. 40:12.)

5. Whom does God declare in his word
Shall ascend to the hill of the Lord?

ALL; hands held outward, then laid on heart. He that hath clean hands and a pure heart. (Ps. 24:4.)

7. *Lift up, lift up,* your hands on high,
Praise God who lives above the sky.

ALL; hands uplifted high. Thus, will I bless thee while I live; I will lift up my hands in thy name. (Ps. 63:4.)

6. Now *clap your hands,* and shout for joy!
In songs of praise your tongues employ.

ALL; clap hands in time. Oh, clap your hands, all ye people; shout unto God with the voice of triumph. (Ps. 47:1.)

Close with hands resting on neighbors' shoulders, interlocked every other one, while a song of praise is sung.

M. G. K.

THE HEAVENLY WAY.

A MOVEMENT EXERCISE.

EXPLANATION OF MOTIONS. 1. Movement with both hands, one after the other, as in going upstairs, to be continued to the end of the line. 2. Point with forefinger of right hand upward. 3. Right hands near the ground, slowly raising till end of line. 4. Movements with both hands as if taking hold of the rounds of a ladder in climbing. 5. Left hands starting at the height at which they naturally hang, raising them gradually in time with the words till the end of line. 6. Hands clasped as in prayer till end of verse. 7. Downward motion with left hands. 8. Both arms starting with wrists at waist, and gradually reaching forward till at arms' length; hold them there till end of verse. 9. Both hands raised gradually upward; all hold each others' hands till end of verse.

1. Climbing, climbing, climbing,[1] the upward road,
Christ is the way, Christ is the way,
The way to heaven; he leads us home to God. [2]

Jesus saith unto him, I am the way. (John 14:6.)

2. Growing, growing, growing,[3] in grace and love;
Oh, let us try! oh, let us try
To grow like him who lives in heaven above. [2]

Grow in grace, and in the knowledge of our Lord and Saviour Jesus Christ. (2 Peter 3:18.)

3. Step after step, step after step,[4] we go;
One at a time, one at a time;
'T is all he asks, the Lord who loves us so.

The steps of a good man are ordered by the Lord. (Ps. 37:23.)

4. Higher, higher, higher,[5] we mount each day,
Jesus we pray, Jesus we pray,[6]
Oh, help us all to climb the heavenly way;

The Lord is my helper. (Heb. 13:6.)

5. Downward, downward, downward,[7] the broad
   road leads;
   Oh, may we ne'er, oh, may we ne'er
   Stray into this, but follow where Christ leads.
   Broad is the way that leads to destruction.
   (Matt. 7:13.)
6. Forward, forward, forward,[8] right straight[8]
   ahead,
   At his command, at his command,
   Who through the sea his ancient people led.
   **Speak unto the children of Israel, that they
   go forward.** (Ex. 14:15.)

7. Upward, upward, upward,[9] unto the end;
   Guide thou our feet, guide thou our feet;[6]
   We shall be safe if we on thee depend.
   **I will instruct thee and teach thee in the
   way which thou shalt go; I will guide thee
   with mine eye.** (Ps. 32:8.)

8. Holding, holding, holding[10] us by the hand,
   Thou Saviour dear, thou Saviour dear;
   Loose not thy clasp till by thy throne we stand.
   Hold thou me up, and I shall be safe. (Ps.
   119:117.)

M. G. K

MOTION BIBLE RECITATIONS.

(Scholars rising at a signal, recite in concert.)

Stand up and bless the Lord your God.
(Neh. 9:5.)

**Lift up your hands in the sanctuary, and
bless the Lord.** (Ps. 134:2.)

O, clap your hands, all ye people. (Ps. 47:1.)

SING, *Clap your hands for joy.* (Chorus.)

She reaches forth her hands unto the needy.
(Prov. 31:20.)

**But when thou doest alms, let not thy left
hand[1] know what thy right hand[2] doeth.**
(Matt. 6:3.)

[1] Hold up left hand, dropping it quickly. [2] Hold up
right hand.

SING, *Freely Give* (one verse).

**Come ye, and let us walk in the light of the
Lord.** (Is. 2:5.) Join hands, keeping step.

**Thy word[1] is a lamp unto my feet,[2] and a
light unto my path.** (Ps. 119:105.)

[1] Point up. [2] Point to feet.

**Hold up my goings in thy paths, that my
footsteps slip not.** (Ps. 17:5). Hands clasped,
eyes closed, heads bowed.

**At the name of Jesus every knee should
bow.** (Phil. 2:10.)

SING, *Precious Name, oh, how sweet.*

**Unto thee lift I up mine eyes, O thou that
dwellest in the heavens.** (Ps. 123:1.)

**Hear,[1] ye children, the instruction of a
father.** (Prov. 4:1.)

[1] Touch ear.

Speak Lord; for thy servant heareth. (1 Sam.
3:9.) Hands clasped, eyes closed, heads bowed.

**Set a watch, O Lord, before my mouth; keep
the door of my lips.** (Ps. 141:3.)

**Keep my commandments, and live; and my
law as the apple of thine eye.**[1]

**Bind them upon thy fingers,[2] write them
upon the table of thine heart.**[3] (Prov. 7:2, 3.)

[1] Touch eye. [2] Revolve hands around each other.
[3] Hand on heart.

**Let not mercy and truth forsake thee; bind
them about thy neck.** (Prov. 3:3.)

Blessings are upon the head of the just.
(Prov. 10:6.)

**My help cometh from the Lord,[1] which made
heaven and earth.**[2] (Ps. 121:2.)

[1] Point up. [2] Point down.

SING, *A Chorus of Praise.*

—*Arranged by E. E. Hewitt.*

BLUE RIBBON BAND.

TEMPERANCE PLEDGE EXERCISE.

Those who have signed the pledge may rise.

TEACHER. What is a pledge?

SCHOLARS. A pledge is a promise.

TEACHER. To whom have we made our Temperance Pledge?

SCH. To God.

TEACHER. How long are we expected to keep
this promise?

SCH. As long as we live.

TEACHER. Into how many parts is our pledge
divided?

SCH. Three.

TEACHER. What do we call such a pledge?
SCH. A triple pledge.

TEACHER. Repeat the pledge or promise we
made to God when we signed our Temperance
Pledge?

SCH. I hereby promise, looking to GOD for
help: That I will try not to buy, sell, give, or
use any drink that has alcohol in it: nor tobacco in any form. Also, that I will not speak
any profane or swearing words.

TEACHER. Recite our pledge prayer.

SCH. Our **Heavenly** Father, hear us now,
     And help us keep this sacred vow;
     Though we are young,
     Oh, make us strong,
     Always to fight against the wrong.

(If preferred, this may be sung. See page 5,
Marching Songs.)

TEACHER. To whom are we to look for help in keeping our pledge?

SCH. To GOD.

TEACHER. What promise of help do we find in his Holy Word?

SCH. He is able to succor them that are tempted.

TEACHER. Those who have kept the pledge may sit down. Those who wish to sign the pledge at the close of the school may rise and repeat the triple pledge. The members of the Band may repeat our prayer for those new members.

Bless those who join our band to-day,
That they may never from thee stray;
Oh, keep them pure; help them to stand
For God, and Home, and Native Land.

SONG, *God always keeps his promises.* Page 64.

TEMPERANCE DOXOLOGY.

(Marching Songs.)

Praise God from whom all blessings flow;
Praise him who heals the drunkard's woe;
Praise him who leads the temperance host;
Praise Father, Son, and Holy Ghost.

M. E. R.

TEMPERANCE SERVICE.

SONG, *Temperance Bells.* Page 62.

BOYS. Who hath woe?

GIRLS. Who hath sorrow?

BOYS. Who hath contentions?

GIRLS. Who hath babblings?

BOYS. Who hath wounds without cause?

GIRLS. Who hath redness of eyes?

BOYS. They that tarry long at the wine.

GIRLS. They that go to seek mixed wine.

BOYS. Look not thou upon the wine when it is red.

GIRLS. When it giveth his color in the cup.

BOYS. When it moveth itself aright.

GIRLS. At the last it biteth like a serpent.

BOYS. And stingeth like an adder.

GIRLS. Wine is a mocker.

BOYS. Strong drink is raging.

ALL. And whosoever is deceived thereby is not wise.

SONG. Page 59.

PRAYER.

OUR TEMPERANCE MOTTO, with motions appropriate to words : —

> TOUCH NOT;
> TASTE NOT;
> HANDLE NOT.

QUESTIONS, WITH BIBLE ANSWERS.

TEACHER. How does Isaiah describe those who drink wine?

SCH. Woe unto them that rise up early in the morning, that they may follow strong drink; that continue until night, till wine inflame them! And the harp and the viol, the tabret and pipe, and wine, are in their feasts : but they regard not the work of the Lord, neither consider the operation of his hands. (Is. 5 : 11, 12.)

TEACHER. What does Solomon teach about strong drink?

SCH. Wine is a mocker, strong drink is raging ; and whosoever is deceived thereby is not wise. (Prov. 20 : 1.)

TEACHER. What does the Bible say we ought to think about?

SCH. Whatsoever things are true, whatsoever things are honest, whatsoever things are pure, whatsoever things are of good report; if there be any virtue, and if there be any praise, think on these things. (Phil. 4 : 8.)

TEACHER. What does the Bible say our bodies are?

SCH. Know ye not that ye are the temple of God, and that the Spirit of God dwelleth in you? If any man destroy the temple of God, him shall God destroy; for the temple of God is holy, which temple ye are. (1 Cor. 3 : 16, 17.)

TEACHER. How does the Bible describe the saloon-keeper?

SCH. He sitteth in the lurking places of the villages; in the secret places doth he murder the innocent. (Ps. 10 : 8.)

TEACHER. What does the Bible say of anyone who offers drink to another?

SCH. Woe unto him that giveth his neighbour drink, that putteth the bottle to him, and maketh him drunken also. (Hab. 2 : 15.)

TEACHER. What does the Bible teach about license?

SCH. Woe to him that buildeth a town with blood, and establisheth a city with iniquity. Better is a little with righteousness, than great revenues without right. (Prov. 16 : 8.)

BOY.

    Who hath red eyes?
    Doth the prophet say
    Aught of that man?
    Can you tell me, pray?

FIRST GIRL.

    'T is he who tarries at the wine;
    Who gives his money, gives his time;
    Who gives his body, gives his soul
    Up to the cruel fiend's control.

BOY.

    Who riseth up at break of day,
    To follow strong drink?
    Doth the prophet say?

SECOND BOY.

    'T is he who seeks the wine that's mixed
    With death; by Satan's wiles 't is fixed;
    That causes tears, and prayers, and sighs —
    The darkest curse below the skies.

BOY.

    But the wine is beautiful in the cup,
    Sending its sparkling bubbles up.

THIRD GIRL.

    Look not upon the red, red wine;
    But pluck the ripe fruit from the vine.
    For the red, red wine in the crystal cup
    Covereth a deadly serpent up.

BOY.

    If I may not drink, then may I sell
    This beverage of which you tell?

FOURTH GIRL.

    Woe unto him who giveth drink,
    Who pusheth a brother over the brink,
    Who putteth a bottle to his lips,
    Who maketh him drunk, as the wine he sips.

ALL, in Concert.

    God's own book is on our side.
    Our sword and shield, whate'er betide.
    We will work and win ere our course is run,
    And keep from the tempter many a one.

RECITATIONS FOR THE LITTLE FOLKS.

BLUE AND RED.

[Lovingly inscribed to the Froebel Loyal Legion.]

BY MRS. ANNA TANNER.

Temperance children in a row,
    Each with a badge of blue;
Toss the ball to and fro,
    That matches the badge in hue.

Brightly blue as the summer sky
    Blue as spring violets;
Throw the ball, but not too high,
    Dainty temperance pets.

Now we'll take another ball
    Red as the blooming rose;
Toss it lightly; don't let it fall,
    Up and down it goes.

Look not on the red, red wine.
    Temperance children true;
With rosy cheeks and eyes that shine,
    Toss both the red and blue.

HOW TO GROW BIG.

How do the pinks and roses grow?
Is it whis-key do you know,
Sprink-led over them each day
Makes them bloom so fresh and gay?
    No, no; let me tell you, no!
    Wa-ter makes the sweet fruits grow:

Rain-drops pat-ter, dew-drops scatter;
So the fresh and cool-ing wa-ter
Wets the vines and trees, and lo!
This is how the flow-ers grow.

How do grapes and ap-ples grow?
Do they all nice jui-ces owe
To cham-pagne, and beer, and ale,
Show-er-ing down on hill and vale?
    No, no; let me tell you, no!
    Wa-ter makes the sweet fruits grow;
Rain-drops pat-ter, dew-drops scat-ter;
So the fresh and cool-ing wa-ter
Wets the vines and trees, and lo!
This is how the sweet fruits grow.

How do lit-tle bird-ies grow,
Fly-ing, singing, chirp-ing so?
Are they fed with wine and rum
In their dain-ty nest-ling home?
    No, no; let me tell you, no!
    Wa-ter makes the bird-ies grow,
Rain-drops pat-ter, dew-drops scatter;
So the fresh and cool-ing wa-ter
Wets their ti-ny beaks, and lo!
That is how the bird-ies grow.

How do lit-tle chil-dren grow?
Not by drink-ing rum. I know;
Bran-dy, ci-der, wine, and beer
Never make them strong and fair.
    No, no; let me tell you, no!
    Wa-ter makes the chil-dren grow,
Rain-drops pat-ter, dew-drops scatter;
Fount-ains fill and flow with wa-ter,
See, they bathe and drink, and lo!
This is how the chil-dren grow.

A GIRL'S SPEECH.

DON'T LEAVE OUT THE GIRLS.

A TEMPERANCE RECITATION.

ROSE.

" Oh, why should little maids unite
　　To join the temperance crew?
How can a little damsel fight
　　Hard drinking to subdue?"

ALICE.

" We want to share the temperance joys —
　　We want a sober heart;
Don't leave all good things to the boys!
　　The girls should have a part.

We want our bodies healthy still,
　　We want a cloudless brain;
We want no weakness of the will —
　　And therefore we abstain.

We want to draw away the crowd
　　That moves on ruin's edge,
And need our warning long and loud;
　　And so we sign the pledge."

ROSE.

" Ah, yes, but who will list to us,
　　Or notice me or you?
'Tis sweet with songs to gather thus,
　　But still what can we do?"

ALICE.

" Why, Rosie, I have read somewhere
　　That woman's power is great;
That woman always has a share
　　Amid the public fate.

The hand of woman can uplift —
　　God helping her — the sad,
And bring to darkest clouds a rift,
　　And make the fallen glad.

The voice of woman tenderly
　　Can lead to love on high;
And women you and I will be
　　As years go fleeting by."

ROSE.

" But, Alice, I don't want to stay
　　Till I 'm a woman tall;
Can you and I do naught to-day
　　To stop the drunkard's fall?"

ALICE.

" Why, yes! a little maiden's word,
　　By loving looks enforced,
Has often better feelings stirred
　　In those the world thought lost.

A tract from out a little hand,
　　For love of Jesus given,
Has guided to the better land,
　　And brought a soul to heaven.

So let us do the work that 's near,
　　And try and trust and pray,
And God will bless us, never fear,
　　And use us day by day."

A BOY'S TEMPERANCE SPEECH.

I propose to consider the temperance cause.

How it has run,
What it has done,
Where it is known,
What is its tone,
Why it has flourished,
How it is nourished.

How has it run?
It has run steadily,
It has run merrily.

What has it done?
It has 'rested the mad,
Reformed the bad,
Refreshed the sad,
Improved the glad;
It has cooled many a lip,
It has saved many a ship.

Where is it known?
In every zone.

What is its tone?
Its tone is inviting,
Its tone is delighting.

Look at our Loyal Temperance Legion. See how happy the children are. See what delight they give to their parents. See the happy families it makes. See the reformed drunkard's wife as her husband in his right mind comes home. See his children as they go to Sunday-school, and the change in himself.

Why has it flourished?
Because it is nourished.

How is it nourished?
By lectures and orations,
By books and illustrations,
By subscriptions and donations,
By glorious expectations.

Now, gentlemen, please bring forward the pledge, and pass around the collection box.

PLEDGE, recited in concert. See page 129.

PLEDGE PRAYER.

PLEDGE SONG. Page 64.

BENEDICTION.

Now unto him that is able to keep you from falling, and to present you faultless before the presence of his glory with exceeding joy, to the only wise God, our Saviour, be glory and majesty, dominion and power, both now and ever. Amen. (Jude 24, 25.)

TEMPERANCE PLEDGES.

WHICH WILL YOU TAKE?

Take your choice of these antidotes to the question, "What will you take?"

NO. 1.

We hereby pledge ourselves, with the help of God, to abstain from the use of all intoxicating liquors as a beverage.

LET THOSE WHO WILL, ADD : From the use of tobacco, and from all profanity.

NO. 2.

Now a solemn pledge we take;
God help us lest that pledge we break.
Rum, gin, and brandy, cider, wine,
Ale, beer, and whiskey, and, in fine,
All liquors that intoxicate
With all our hearts we'll always hate;
We'll neither drink, buy, sell, nor give,
A single drop as long as we live.

NO. 3.

" I don't think,
That I ever will drink,
Brandy or gin,
Whiskey or rum:
Or any other thing
That will make drunk come!"

NO. 4.

"I WILL TRY" PLEDGE.

I hereby promise, LOOKING TO GOD FOR HELP, *that I will try —*
Not to buy, sell, give, or use any drink that will intoxicate.
Nor tobacco in any form.
Also, that I will not speak any profane or swearing word.

May God help you to keep this pledge which makes you a member of the

BLUE RIBBON BAND

OF THE

———————Primary Class.

———————*Teacher.*

A REASON FOR TRYING NOW.

From very little boys have grown
The greatest men the world has known;
From very little girls have grown
The noblest women ever known.

NO. 5.

Never shall these two little lips of mine,
Taste anything at all like wine.

NO. 6.

We do pledge, in God's fear,
Not to smoke nor to swear;
And we'll never drink cider or beer
Anywhere!

NO. 7.

THE PLEDGE OF THE CHILDREN OF THE BAND OF HOPE.

We are pledged that no marks of profaneness
Defacing life's record shall come,
No worshipful service be rendered
To kings of Tobacco and Rum;
But to sow in their fields of destruction
The pearl-seed of mercy and right,
For our Saviour to treasure with jewels
He keeps in the Kingdom of Light.

We will cull the first beautiful blossoms
To lay on the altar of love,
And the fragrance from censers ascending
Shall float to the angels above.
May our vows with the incense we offer
Acceptably blend in his sight,
When our Saviour receiveth the jewels
We bear to the Kingdom of Light.

Ever free from the taint of the winecup,
Our lips shall be lifted in praise.
And our hands from its crimson-bound fetters
Unshackled towards heaven we raise:
They are cleansed from the touch that defileth,
To serve in the beauty of might.
When our Saviour shall call for his jewels,
To wear in the Kingdom of Light.

NO. 8.

Temperance pledge used by an Endeavor society in Kansas City:

Trusting in the Lord Jesus Christ for strength, I promise him that I will drink no intoxicating liquor; that I will use no tobacco; that I will use no profane language; that I will never listen to or repeat an impure story (Read Matt. 5:8; 1 Cor. 3:16, 17); and I will pray each day that the saloon may be banished from our land, and just as far as I know how I will work for what I pray, and I will also vote as I pray, and do all in my power to help kill "King Alcohol."

OFFERING SERVICES.

A COLLECTION EXERCISE.

Each child is provided with the appropriate letter, which is turned toward the audience as the recitation is given.

My letter stands for the cry of the needy.
C—ome over into Macedonia and help us.

My letter calls for an offering.
O—ffer unto God thanksgiving, and pay thy vows unto the Most High.

My letter gives direction to our love.
L—ove not the world, neither the things that are in the world.

My letter calls for an *exhibition* of love.
L—et us not love in word, neither in tongue; but in deed and in truth.

My letter teaches the spirit of giving.
E—very man as he purposeth in his heart, so let him give; not grudgingly or of necessity; for God loveth a cheerful giver.

My letter teaches us to give in faith.
C—ast thy bread upon the waters; for thou shalt find it after many days.

My letter stands for a proof we are slow to believe.
T—he love of money is the root of all evil.

My letter promises success to missionary efforts.
I—will give thee the heathen for thine inheritance, and the uttermost parts of the earth for thy possession.

My letter is an invitation to exalt the name of the Lord.
O—h, magnify the Lord with me, and let us exalt his name together.

My letter completes the word and gives God the glory.
N—ow unto him that is able to keep you from falling, and to present you faultless before the presence of his glory with exceeding joy, to the only wise God, our Saviour, be glory and majesty, dominion and power, both now and ever. Amen.

SHOW YOUR LOVE.

A recitation before a collection.

Dear friends, have you had a good time?
How do you like this school of mine?
Don't all speak at once. Wait till I show
The right way to answer, you know.
If you love us, let us know it.
This is the way you should show it —
Just hand a little money out
And that will settle every doubt.

Are you glad that you came to-night?
And pleased with what has met your sight?
Then don't you think you ought to pay
For it before you go away?

If you think so, let us know it.
We'll tell you how you can show it —
Just hand a little money out
And that will settle every doubt.

Why do I say these things to you?
Ah, well! I have an end in view.
Actions speak louder than words, they say,
That is why we ask you to-day :—
If you love us, how shall we know it?
Dear parents, *show it, show* it !
Just hand a little money out,
And that will settle every doubt.

M. G. K.

CHAPEL BUILDERS.

Offerings on Children's Day, Easter, Christmas, or any missionary occasion may be enclosed in boxes shaped and colored like bricks, which cost about $2 to $3 per hundred. Lay as a foundation a large box; as the boxes are brought up, a boy should build them into a chapel. A roof with a steeple may be made of cardboard; a bell may be hung in the steeple. The verses below were written for a mission band jubilee, where the offerings were used toward a chapel in Africa.

"Except the Lord build the house, they labour in vain that build it."

We ask thee now, our Father,
To bless what we have done;
Increase our little offerings,
A hundredfold each one.

May pennies grow to dollars,
Each dollar earn a score,
And ev'ry twenty dollars
As much again or more.

We've laid a sure foundation
In love to Christ our King;
And by his power he'll stablish
What we in weakness bring.

Upon this strong foundation
We've built with utmost care,
Setting each brick with patience,
Securing it with prayer.

But as this little chapel
Unroofed is no avail,
So is our offering useless
If thy rich blessing fail.

As we complete our chapel
Putting its roof in place,
Do thou send down thy blessing,
Enlarge us by thy grace.

— *Elizabeth M. Rawlings.*

SING. TUNE: *Little Builders*, page 28.

One by one the stones we lay,
Building slowly day by day.
Building by our love are we
In the lands beyond the sea;
Building by each thought and prayer
For the souls that suffer there;
Building in the Hindu land,
Where the idols are as sand.

Building in vast China too,
Living temples rise to view;
Building in Japan as well:
Ah, what stories we could tell!
Building on dark Afric's shore,
That there may be slaves no more;
Living stones we helped to bring
For the palace of our King.

AN OFFERING DRILL.

Suitable for Anniversaries, Missionary Meetings, or other occasion at which a collection is to be taken.

Music. — All the hymns are from Gospel Hymns. Any suitable march.

Seventeen girls are needed. *Eight little girls* about eight or nine years old. Four of these should be dressed in pink, and four in blue, each bearing over her right shoulder a *sickle* wound with the same color as the dress.

Eight larger girls, about twelve or thirteen years old, dressed in white; each bearing a rake painted white, and having a bag attached made of white cotton goods gathered around a wire ring.

A Captain, who carries a banner.

The captain leads the girls in white (without their rakes) across the platform, until they form a line at the back. *Captain* then gives the orders — " Forward — march ! " The line advances to the centre of the platform, and sings with appropriate motions one stanza of " Sowing the Seed," No. 79, Gospel Hymns.

Captain orders: " Right face — forward — march ! " Leads them out, and returns at the head of the smaller girls. Proceed as before, and sing one stanza of " Oh, where are the Reapers?" No. 155. Sickles to be changed from one shoulder to the other on the words *garner*, *sickles*, *reapers*, and *garner*.

While these are singing the last line, the larger girls enter, with rakes over right shoulder, and take position behind the others; the two lines being several feet apart.

Captain. " Reapers, right about face ! " Little girls turn, four to right and four to left, lines facing.

SONG, Gospel Hymns, No. 33.

FIRST ROW.

Weary gleaner, whence comest thou,
With empty hands and clouded brow?
Plodding along thy lonely way,
Tell me where thou hast gleaned to-day.

SECOND ROW.

Late I found a barren field.
The harvest past my search revealed;
Others golden sheaves had gained;
Only stubble for me remained.

FIRST ROW.

Forth to the harvest field away !
Gather your handfuls while you may;
All day long in the fields abide,
Gleaning close by the reapers' side.

Captain. " Reapers, right and left face !" Little girls turn to front.

Captain. " Right face — forward — march." Now follows any pretty march, occupying from five to ten minutes. With sixteen, a number of pretty figures can be produced. This should end with the two lines in *position*.

The Captain then steps forward and makes a speech suited to the occasion, stating the object for which the offering is to be taken.

Captain gives the order: " *Gleaners*, right face — forward — march ! " Gleaners march off the stage, leaving reapers standing. Each gleaner takes position at the head of an aisle previously assigned. When all are stationed, they proceed to take the collection in the bags on the rakes. They return to the platform, singing " Bringing in the Sheaves." Then the entire company, winding in and out, marches off, still singing the refrain " Bringing in the sheaves " till the sound is lost in the distance.

FORGET ME NOT BAND.

MEETINGS OF THE BAND.

Held monthly, in connection with the Sabbath session, or on   afternoon at   o'clock. At this time reports are read by the children, exercises and items of interest pertaining to the work given, and a collection taken.

OBJECT OF THE BAND.

To ascertain the names of the sick of our church and school, first of all, then so far as possible to extend to others, and take to them remembrances of fruit or flowers, picture cards and booklets.

A COMMITTEE

Known as the "Distributing Committee," to carry the offerings to the sick, is selected from the older boys and girls in the advanced classes of our Primary Department.

BAND TEXT.

Inasmuch as ye have done it unto one of the least of these my brethren, ye have done it unto me.

MOTTO.

For Jesus' sake,
Do all the good you can,
To all the people you can,
At all the times you can,
In all the ways you can,
As long as ever you can.

THE SUPPORT OF THE BAND.

This is through our BIRTHDAY BOX, into which the scholars drop at least as many pennies as they are years old, each year as their birthdays occur. Also by our annual social.

OUR HYMN.

For our pleasant birthdays,
　　Lord, we gladly sing;
For our years so happy,
　　Lord, we gladly bring.

Many little children
　　Now are sick and sad;
These we will remember,
　　Help to make them glad.

OUR WORK.

The little waterdrops come down
　　To make the flowers grow;
The little rivulets flow on
　　To bless where'er they go;
The little seeds make mighty trees
　　To cool us with their shade;
If little things like these do good,
　　To try I'm not afraid.
We all may work for Jesus,
　　Wherever we may be;
I'll try to work for Jesus,
　　Who did so much for me.

M. E. R.

HOME MISSIONS.

TEACHER. What is meant by Home Missions?
SCH. Missions in our own land.

TEACHER. Who that come to this country from lands called Christian need the services of Home Mission societies?
SCH. European immigrants.

TEACHER. What people of another race, living here in great numbers, need its services?
SCH. The Negroes.

TEACHER. Who also need help who are considered the wards of our government?
SCH. The Indians.

TEACHER. What people under the United States government are ignorant of God?
SCH. The inhabitants of Alaska.

TEACHER. What people are bound by fearful error, although supposed to know of God?
SCH. The Mormons.

TEACHER. Who come to us from heathen shores?
SCH. The Chinese.

TEACHER. Among what people, nominally Christian, but in fact almost as darkened as the heathen, have we a few missionaries?
SCH. The Mexicans.

— *Missionary Instruction.*

BEGINNING WITH AMERICA.

[Teacher, read or tell the story of the day of Pentecost.]

TEACHER. There are some things in this story that make me think of our country. People from how many nations had gathered at Jerusalem?
SCH. Fourteen nations.

TEACHER. Do you know how many nations are represented among the people in the United States?
SCH. There are said to be about one hundred different languages spoken in the United States by people coming to this country from foreign lands.

TEACHER. Are the foreigners who come to our country Christians?
SCH. Very few of them are real Christians.

TEACHER. Are all of our own people Christians?
SCH. No; and altogether there are a great many more people in our land who do not truly know and worship God than there are real Christians.

TEACHER. So although we call our country a Christian land, there are many people in it who are practically heathen. We will now listen to a recitation called —

OUR HEATHEN AT HOME.

I do not propose your attention to take
From the *foreign heathen's* condition;
But allow me a brief appeal to make
For the needs of our wide *Home Mission.*

In a general way, my friends, you know,
This wonderful Yankee nation
Is going ahead, and is bound to go
In the van of all creation.

I cannot spare words, and you cannot spare time,
For each national perfection.
Though you know I could reel a ream of rhyme
On the glories of each section.

But people, you know, are inclined to dwell
With rather too much satisfaction,
On what *has been done* that is wise and well,
To the hindrance of further action.

Now it seems to me that is just the way
With our satisfied Yankee nation;
So permit me to hint a few things to-day,
That may check your self-gratulation.

First we opened our doors to the "Heathen Chinee,"
With his labor — and idols we have him;
We count up the value his labor will be;
Do we try from his idols to save him?

And next there is Utah, as full of sin
As any Mohammedan nation;
Are we sending St. Paul's sort of bishops in
To establish a mission station?

We are teaching the Hindus the fearful wrong
Of throwing babes into the waters,
While some Indian tribes to our own land belong
Who are killing their baby daughters.

These wild tribes our troops are destroying so fast,
They have souls, have they not? Will it be, then,
A wise Christian plan to leave them till the last,
While we labor for far foreign heathen?

So a voice seems to sound from North, South, East, and West,
"This do, nor leave undone the other!"
Nor claim as a land to be very first-best,
While such are our sisters and brothers.

There is much to be done with work, wealth, heart, and hand
In this heathenish conglomeration,
Before we can fairly consider our land
A civilized, Christianized nation.

"What is everyone's work is nobody's," they say,
There is work to be done, and we know it.
Let us take a fresh start, and devise the best way
To do good to these folks, *and then do it.*

TEACHER. So, we see, there is much to be done in preaching the gospel to our home heathen, and this, not only that they may be saved, but that they may tell others of the way of salvation, and thus glorify Jesus. To which of the nations represented at Jerusalem do you think the three thousand belonged who believed and were baptized?

SCH. **Some to each nation.**

TEACHER. Without doubt. What do you suppose these believers did when they went back to their own countries?

SCH. **Told what they had heard in Jerusalem.**

TEACHER. Just so; and here you see one way in which, in a very short time, the gospel was preached to fourteen nations, beginning at Jerusalem. In this same way to how many nations might the gospel be preached, beginning in North America?

SCH. **To as many nations as have representatives in North America.**

TEACHER. What must be done first?

SCH. **The story must be told to these foreign speaking people in languages they can understand.**

TEACHER. And when these foreigners have heard in our land this story and believe it with all their hearts, what then?

SCH. **Some of them will go back to the countries from which they came, carrying the good news, and so shall the gospel be preached in many lands, beginning with America.**

TEACHER.

We will now rise and sing:

To prairie homes and Western wilds
We'll send the gospel story,
And in its beams to darkened souls
Reveal a Saviour's glory.

REFRAIN.

And each to each a welcome give
With true and earnest greeting.
One Lord, one faith, one purpose true,
Our hearts are as one beating.

O God, speed on thy chariot wheels,
Till through our land and nation
From sea to sea, from shore to shore,
All know the great salvation

From MISSIONARY GARDENERS; Home Mission Lessons for Boys and Girls. By Mary G. Burdette, 2411 Indiana Avenue, Chicago. In this little book are instructive lessons about the Indians, colored people, and the foreigners who come to our land.

MISSIONARY SERVICE.

"GO YE."

INTRODUCTION.

SING, *Whosoever will.* Gospel Hymns, No. 1.

TEACHER. 1. What does the word *foreign* mean?

SCH. The word "foreign" means not of one's own country.

TEACHER. 2. What does *missionary* mean?

SCH. "Missionary" means one sent.

TEACHER. 3. Then what is a *Christian foreign missionary*?

SCH. A Christian foreign missionary is one who is sent to other lands to tell the "good tidings" of salvation through Jesus.

TEACHER. 4. By whose commands are these missionaries sent?

SCH. By the command of our Lord Jesus Christ, given just before his ascension into heaven.

TEACHER. 5. Repeat this command.

SCH. "Go ye into all the world, and preach the gospel to every creature" (Mark 16:15).

SING, *Hear the voice of Jesus crying,* one verse. Gospel Hymns, No. 1.

TEACHER. 7. Whom did the Lord Jesus mean when he said "Go ye"?

SCH. He meant everybody; every Christian man, woman, and child should take some part in the work of foreign missions.

TEACHER. 8. Can we all go to other lands?

SCH. No, not all; but we can work for Jesus at home, and help those who do go to foreign lands.

SING, *What can I do for Jesus?* Page 82.

TEACHER. 10. How can we help those who go?

SCH. By our gifts, our prayers, and our loving sympathy.

TEACHER. 11. Why is *money* needed for this work?

SCH. Money is needed for the support of the missionaries; for building churches, hospitals, and schools; for publishing Bibles, and other Christian books, and for many other good purposes.

TEACHER. 12. Repeat some Bible words about giving.

GIRLS. "Freely ye have received; freely give."

BOYS. "God loveth a cheerful giver."

SING, *Freely Give.* Page 48.

TEACHER. 14. Why should we *pray* for missions?

GIRLS. The missionaries say, "Pray for us."

BOYS. Jesus says: "Without me, ye can do nothing."

SCH. God's promise is, "Ask of me, and I shall give thee the heathen for thine inheritance, and the uttermost parts of the earth for thy possessions."

TEACHER. 15. Why should we feel a loving sympathy?

SCH. Because the work of missions honors the Lord Jesus, and aims to save souls.

SING, *Loving and Giving.* Page 51.

TEACHER. 17. How can we increase our interest?

SCH. By attending missionary meetings: by learning more of the work; and by loving the Lord Jesus more and more ourselves.

TEACHER. 18. What precious words did the Lord Jesus say when he gave the command "Go ye"?

GIRLS. "All power is given unto me, in heaven and in earth."

BOYS. "Lo, I am with you alway, even unto the end of the world."

TEACHER. 19. Then what *must* be the result of this work?

SCH. God says: "The earth shall be filled with the glory of the knowledge of the Lord, as the waters cover the sea."

Recited as a prayer with bowed heads.

SCH. "Blessed be his glorious name forever, and let the whole world be filled with his glory. Amen, and amen."

SING.

> Let every nation, every tribe,
> On this terrestrial ball,
> To him all majesty ascribe,
> And crown him Lord of all.

L. E. H.

IDOLS.

Arrange your children so that they may be *seen* in a semicircle, pyramid, or other pretty shape. Remember that the beauty of a movement-exercise depends on the exactness and uniformity of the motions. One little hand raised out of time will spoil all as effectually as a note out of tune. But children love these action pieces, and are very easily trained to perfect unison.

Start with folded hands, or arms crossed on bosom. In both the *psalm* and *song*, the motions are similar. At the word *heathen* or *far-off*, extend arms at full length toward the east; at *God*, point upward; *heavens*, both hands raised; the work of *men's hands*, hammering motion;

touch eyes, ears, mouth, throat, etc., as each part is named.

For the passage in Isaiah have several *boys*. They will fall naturally into the various motions of the blacksmith and carpenter, hewing and planing of trees, warming hands at the fire kindled from the lopped-off branches, etc. From the words "*He is hungry*" to "*and is faint*," let the voice grow fainter and fainter, the head droop, and the whole attitude be one of complete exhaustion.

"If the Lord be God, follow him; but if Baal, then follow him."

SINGLE VOICE.

Children, do you the story know
Of idol gods? And can you show
What they are like, and by whose hands
Are formed the gods of heathen lands?

RECITATIONS by the class, of Psalm 115:2-8, with motions.

Wherefore should the heathen say, Where is now their God? But our God is in the heavens: he hath done whatsoever he hath pleased. Their idols are silver and gold, the work of men's hands. They have mouths, but they speak not: eyes have they, but they see not: They have ears, but they hear not: noses they have, but they smell not: They have hands, but they handle not: feet have they, but they walk not: neither speak they through their throats. They that make them are like unto them; so is every one that trusteth in them.

King David in his *Psalms* hath told
Their idols silver are and gold,
Only the work of human *hands*,
These gods of *far-off* heathen lands.

CHORUS.

Our God is in the *heavens above*,
We'll *praise* him with full *hearts* of love,
We'll shout hosannas to his name,
While *heaven* and *earth* his power proclaim.

They all have *mouths*, but cannot talk;
They all have *feet*, but cannot walk;
Two *eyes* that cannot see have they;
A *tongue* that not a word can say.

Two *ears* that ne'er a sound have heard;
Hands, that for work have never stirred;
Each has a *nose* that cannot smell;
A *throat* through which no note doth swell.

So every one that trusteth them,
These worthless idols, *wrought* by men,
They, too, who make them with their *hands*
Are like these gods of heathen lands.

RECITATION, with motions, of Isaiah 44:12-20.

The smith with the tongs both worketh in the coals, and fashioneth it with hammers, and worketh it with the strength of his arms: yea, he is hungry, and his strength faileth: he drinketh no water, and is faint. The carpenter stretcheth out his rule; he marketh it out with a line: he fitteth it with plans, and he marketh it out with the compass, and maketh it after the figure of a man, according to the beauty of a man: that it may remain in the house. He heweth him down cedars, and taketh the cypress and the oak, which he strengtheneth for himself among the trees of the forest: he planteth an ash, and the rain doth nourish it. Then shall it be for a man to burn: for he will take thereof, and warm himself; yea, he kindleth it, and baketh bread; yea, he maketh a god, and worshipeth it; he maketh it a graven image, and falleth down thereto. He burneth part thereof in the fire; with part thereof he eateth flesh; he roasteth roast and is satisfied: yea, he warmeth himself, and saith, Aha, I am warm, I have seen the fire: and the residue thereof he maketh a god, even his graven image: he falleth down unto it, and worshippeth it, and prayeth unto it, and saith, Deliver me; for thou art my god. They have not known or understood: for he hath shut their eyes, that they cannot see; and their hearts, that they cannot understand. And none considereth in his heart, neither is there knowledge nor understanding to say, I have burned part of it in the fire; yea, also I have baked bread upon the coals thereof; I have roasted flesh and eaten it: and shall I make the residue thereof an abomination? shall I fall down to the stock of a tree? He feedeth on ashes: a deceived heart hath turned him aside, that he cannot deliver his soul, nor say, Is there not a lie in my right hand?

SINGLE VOICE.

Now folded be your little hands,
Then altogether you may tell
How unlike gods of heathen lands
Is our great God we love so well.

If we our *love* to him confess,
He will be mindful us to bless;
He has enough to spare for *all*,
Holds *wide his arms* to *great* and *small*.

What priceless blessings thus are given
By him who made both *earth* and *heaven!*
The *earth* for man to dwell on gave,
In *heaven* he waits our souls to save.

Oh, let us *praise* him with each breath,
Before our *eyelids* close in death,
Too late 't is then to sing his praise;
But now to him glad songs we'll raise.

M. G. K.

GOOD TIDINGS.

A FLAG EXERCISE FOR MISSION BANDS.

BY MISS EMMA F. R. CAMPBELL.

[*By permission* of Woman's Foreign Missionary Society Presbyterian Church, 1334 Chestnut Street, Philadelphia.]

DIRECTIONS.

Have prepared a good-sized flag of each of the nations represented. Also a banner made of crimson material with a white cross in the centre; adding, if desired, above and below, the words of the motto. "By this —— we conquer." Select enough boys and girls with good voices to take the different parts; one of the best speakers to remain in the room prepared to go on the platform at the proper time to address the others, who with their flags, and headed by one carrying the banner, will enter the church and march slowly up the aisle, singing the following hymn, the whole Band joining in the chorus.

BANNER HYMN. Tune 116, *Gospel Hymns, No. 5.*

There 's a royal banner given for display
　To the soldiers of the King:
As an ensign fair we lift it up to-day,
　While as ransomed ones we sing.

CHORUS.

Marching on! Marching on!
　For Christ count everything but loss:
And to crown him King, toil and sing,
　'Neath the banner of the cross.

Over land and sea, wherever man may dwell,
　Make the glorious tidings known;
Of the crimson banner now the story tell,
　While the Lord shall claim his own! — CHO.

When the glory dawns — 't is dawning very near—
　It is hastening day by day —
Then before our King the foe shall disappear,
　And the Cross the world shall sway. — CHO.

As they reach the desk or platform, let them divide and stand on each side so as to face the audience while they finish the hymn; then the leader, with the banner, will step out a little in front, and respond to the questions of the boy on the platform, each reciting alternate verses of the following poem: —

BOY.

What news? What tidings bring ye? How goes
　the fight? Who win?
Whose colors are triumphant? Whose hath the
　battle been?
Say, hath the royal ensign that bears the kingly
　name
In which the Cross is woven known victory or
　shame?

LEADER.

He giveth us the victory, through him once given
　for all!
Before that blood-bought standard the hosts of
　darkness fall!
The echoing trumpets rock the walls ere seven
　times girdled round —
The everlasting hills awake, the ocean hears the
　sound.

BOY.

Hark! Is not that a murmur like a far-off moun-
　tain stream
That sings of sunny hillsides? See! Is not that
　the gleam
Of scythe and sickle? Surely 't is a song! Do
　ye not hear?
Ho! reapers, ye come singing! What cheer,
　good friends, what cheer?

LEADER.

"Lift up your eyes," they answer; "the fields
　stretch fair and wide,
Already white, and waiting the glorious harvest-
　tide!
Lo, as the crown of Lebanon the mighty harvests
　shake,
Sown where the blood-drenched land the feet of
　trampling armies brake!"

BOY.

Look! Where yon mountain flushes beneath
　dawn's kisses sweet,
Winged with "glad tidings of great joy," behold
　their pilgrim feet.
Whence come ye? whither haste ye? From what
　blest country far,
Bring ye those mystic branches? Oh, say from
　whence ye are.

LEADER.

With olive branches [1] laden, we bring glad news
　of peace:
We come, ambassadors of One whose kingdom
　shall not cease!
We go, where bound with many chains, in inner
　prisons, wait
Those who have never heard his name — earth's
　children desolate.

[1] Branches of evergreen may be substituted for the flags, or attached to them in some way.

BOY.

God speed you ! May the desert-place before you
burst to bloom !
Christ keep you ! May the living Light flash swift
athwart the gloom !
Hosanna in the highest ! for the Lord our God
doth reign,
Omnipotent, eternal ! Yea, " He lives, who once
was slain ! "
— *Rose Angel.*

After this recitation, let the boy with the banner go up and take his position in the middle of
the platform, while the others come up in turn,
read or recite short sketches of the progress of
the work in different countries, and range them-
selves on each side, according to size, forming,
when all are through, a semicircle of children
and flags, making a beautiful tableau. As they
stand, let the organ or piano play a prelude and
accompaniment for the following hymn; those
on the platform singing the verse, all the Band
joining in the chorus.

(*Missionary Hymnal.* Tune 18.)

A highway we are building for the ransomed of
the Lord ;
With the Cross for its foundation and its arches
in the Word,
It shall bridge the widest chasms with the promises of God.
Whose kingdom marches on.

CHORUS.

Glory, glory, hallelujah !
God's kingdom marches on.

Across the mighty continents and o'er the path-
less sea
We are stretching massive arches that shall last
eternally,
And along the shining pathway press the footsteps of the free;
God's kingdom marches on. — CHO.

From Orient and Occident these children of a
King
To claim a royal heritage their souls from bond-
age bring,
And as they seek their Father's House, their
happy voices sing —
God's kingdom marches on. — CHO.

Piano will play while those on the platform
come down and take their seats. Or it may close
with the following Flag Drill.

FLAG DRILL.

For sixteen girls, each with a flag of some heathen nation. They may march on the platform,
making as many pretty figures as you wish,
weaving the children in four lines. Then follows the drill, which has a beautiful effect.

1. Form semicircle, with two girls in centre,
one kneeling and one standing. To do this only
those in the inner lines need to move.
2. All flags to right.
3. All flags to left.
4. All to centre.
5. All from centre.
6. Columns face.
7. Inside columns face, and outside face outward.
8. Four flags crossed. The girls in columns
one and two, and those in columns three and
four, who are diagonally opposite, being num-
bered from one to four, thus : 2 4
9. Eight flags crossed.   3 1
10. Circle form around one girl, all facing in,
and flags raised and touching.
11. All face outward, and back to original
place.
12. Countermarch from platform.

N. B. — A child as captain, with an American
flag, may give the orders. After each command
they return to original position in four lines.

OBJECTS OF WORSHIP.

TEACHER. 1. What proportion of the inhab-
itants of the earth have heard of Christ?
SCH. **About one third.**
TEACHER. 2. Who are called nominal Chris-
tians?
SCH. **Those who believe the Bible.**
TEACHER. 3. Who only are true Christians,
and will be saved through Christ?
SCH. **Those who from their hearts accept
him as their Saviour and Lord.**
TEACHER. 4. Who besides Protestants are
nominal Christians?
SCH. **Roman Catholics and the Greek Church.**
TEACHER. 5. What people accept the Old, but
not the New Testament?
SCH. **The Jews or Israelites.**
TEACHER. 6. What do we call those who do
not know of our God and Saviour?
SCH. **Heathen.**
TEACHER. 7. What people believe in one God,
but not in the Saviour, and discard the Bible?
SCH. **The Mohammedans.**
TEACHER. 8. What have been most generally
worshiped by heathen?
SCH. **Certain objects in nature, especially the
sun.**
TEACHER. 9. What other objects?
SCH. **Certain animals.**
TEACHER. 10. What besides these?
SCH. **Images, called idols.**

TEACHER. 11. Where are idols still worshiped?

SCH. In Burma, India, China, Japan, and a few other countries.

TEACHER. 12. The only idea of worship that some heathen people in these lands have is the giving of offerings to appease anger and avert trouble. In this sense of the word, what do many worship who are not idolaters?

SCH. Evil spirits or demons.

TEACHER. 13. What are the principal systems of idol-worship in Asia?

SCH. Brahmanism (Brah-man-ism) and Buddhism (Bood-ism).

TEACHER. 14. To what besides idols do the Chinese offer worship?

SCH. Their dead ancestors.

TEACHER. 15. What do the lowest heathen worship?

SCH. Fetiches (fe'tish-es).

TEACHER. 16. What are fetiches?

SCH. Charms; certain things, sometimes natural objects, sometimes made by men, sometimes idols, which are supposed to possess a supernatural power.

TEACHER. 17. Where are fetiches still worshiped?

SCH. In Africa and some of the Pacific Isles.

FOREIGN MISSION BANDS.

Each child holds a letter of flowers, evergreen or gilt cardboard, forming the words FOREIGN MISSION BANDS. As each verse is recited those holding the letters forming the words in capitals, step out from the line, moving back when their verse is spoken.

SING, *Loving and Giving.* Page 5.

ALL.

We are only little children,
But we long to serve our King.
In his Word he clearly shows us
Just what service we may bring.

So we read the words of Jesus,
Then the Master's voice is heard
Whispering softly, "Little children,
Be ye DOERS of the Word."

We can only do a little,
But that little blessed will be,
For our Jesus says, "A wee thing
Done in love is done FOR ME."

There are many little children
Knowing nought of love divine,
But our loving heavenly Father
Says, "These children too are MINE."

And he bids us GO and teach them
Of the Father kind and good,
And of Christ who came to save them
By the shedding of his blood.

But, you know, such little children
Cannot go to far-off lands,
So we'll try to SEND the message

ALL—

Through our FOREIGN MISSION
BANDS.

From the place of his habitation, he looketh upon all the inhabitants of the earth.

O Lord, our Lord, how excellent is thy name in all the earth!

Righteousness and judgment are the habitation of his throne.

Enter into his gates with thanksgiving, and into his courts with praise.

In his hand are the deep places of the earth: the strength of the hills is his also.

Great is the Lord, and greatly to be praised.

Now, Lord, what wait I for? My hope is in thee.

Make a joyful noise unto the Lord, all ye lands.
Serve the Lord with gladness.

In God we boast all the day long, and praise thy name forever.

Sing unto God, ye kingdoms of the earth; Oh, sing praises unto the Lord.

Surely his salvation is nigh them that fear him: that glory may dwell in our lands.

I will hear what God the Lord will speak; for he will speak peace unto his people.

O God, the heathen are come into thine inheritance.

None of them can by any means redeem his brother.

But thou, O Lord God of hosts, awake to visit all the heathen.

All the ends of the world shall remember and turn unto the Lord. And all the kindreds of the nations shall worship before thee.

Now know I that the Lord saveth.

Day unto day uttereth speech and night unto night showeth knowledge.

Salvation belongeth unto the Lord: thy blessing is upon thy people.

—*E. M. Rawlings.*

THE CHRISTIAN ARMOR.

BOYS, each holding a piece of armor made from pasteboard covered with silver paper, march on singing MARCHING SONG, page 8. Let each as he recites his verse and text hold up his armor; if he can then *put it on*, it will add to the effect.

NO. 1.

Go put on God's armor,
And stand in the fight;
So weak in thine own strength,
But strong in his might.

Be strong in the Lord, and in the power of his might. Put on the whole armour of God, that ye may be able to stand against the wiles of the devil. (Eph. 6: 10, 11.)

NO. 2.

The *Girdle of Truth*
Put about thee with care,
And strengthen it daily
By watching and prayer.

Stand therefore, having your loins girt about with truth.

NO. 3.

Thy *breastplate*,
Can only of righteousness be,
And that the Lord Jesus
Will give unto thee.

Having on the breastplate of righteousness.

Thy feet must *be shod*,
With the gospel of peace.
His message ye carry,
His praise must not cease.

And your feet shod with the preparation of the gospel of peace.

NO. 4.

And then to protect thee
Take Faith's brightest *shield;*
'T will break all the weapons
The wicked can wield.

Above all taking the shield of Faith, wherewith ye shall be able to quench all the fiery darts of the wicked.

NO. 5.

Thy helmet. salvation,
The gift of our Lord;
Fight bravely for Jesus
And he will reward.

And take the helmet of salvation.

NO. 6.

The *sword* of the Spirit,
Thy weapon shall be;
The word of our God
Makes the enemy flee.

And the sword of the Spirit which is the word of God.

NO. 7.

The foes are about thee,
Without and within;
Go forth thus accoutred,
And conquer all sin.

Praying always with all prayer and supplication in the Spirit, and watching thereunto with all perseverance.

SINGING BY THE CLASS. *Happy Little Soldiers.* Page 88.

THOU, GOD, SEEST ME.

FOR FOUR LITTLE GIRLS.

Each may have a banner with the word of the text on one side, and the duty on the other. For instance: No. 1.—THOU on one side, and FOLLOW on reverse.

THOU, my God, art ever present,
Ever watchful over me;
Thou dost lead in ways most pleasant,
Let me ever *follow* thee.

GOD, my Father, I would *serve* thee,
Ev'ry moment, all my days;
In thy tenderness preserve me,
Teach my lips to speak thy praise.

SEEST thou that I do *love* thee?
My dear Lord, I love thee so;
More than aught in skies above me,
More than aught in earth below.

ME the Lord hath ever guided;
I would ever *trust* his Word;
All to him I have confided;
I will honor thee, my Lord.

ALL.

Yes, we 'll *follow* Jesus,
Serve him day by day;
Love him first and always,
Trust in him for aye.
Let us each remember,
His we are to be;
And our Lord is watching;
THOU, GOD, SEEST ME.

E. M. R.

THE VOICE OF THE CLOCK.

BY MRS. M. G. KENNEDY.

For twelve children ranged in a semicircle. They swing their arms backward and forward like a pendulum, in exact time at each "tick, tock," and count each hour in its turn in a slow measure, in the precise time of the ticking. The beauty depends on the exactness.

It will be still more effective if a large clock face is prepared from pasteboard; the hands may be moved from behind, and made to correspond with the hour which is being spoken of. A bell may also be made to strike the number of hours.

TOGETHER.

Tick, tock, tick, tock, tick, tock,
  Come and hear the voice of this clock;
Learn its lessons, as day by day
  It ticks the passing hours away:
Tick, tock, tick, tock, tick, tock,
  One!

FIRST CHILD.

One God there is in heaven above,
  One Lord and Saviour, Jesus Christ;
One Holy Spirit, sent in love,
  One heavenly Father, over all.

TOGETHER.

Tick, tock, tick, tock, tick, tock,
  One, two!

SECOND CHILD.

Two commandments has Jesus given,
  Two laws, on which hang all the rest;
Love the Lord thy God in heaven,
  And love thy neighbor as thyself.

TOGETHER.

Tick, tock, tick, tock, tick, tock,
  One, two, three!

THIRD CHILD.

Three persons, who are yet but one,
  Is the great God whom we adore,
The Father, Spirit, and the Son;
  These three are one, that one is God.

TOGETHER.

Tick, tock, tick, tock, tick, tock,
  One, two, three, four!

FOURTH CHILD.

Four seasons in their course do run,
  Spring, Summer, Autumn, Winter, these
The Lord hath promised all shall come,
  While earth remains they shall not cease.

TOGETHER.

Tick, tock, tick, tock, tick, tock,
  One, two, three, four, five!

FIFTH CHILD.

Five virgins wise, whose lamps burn bright,
  Hasten forth to meet the bridegroom,
But five had lamps that would not light;
  They came too late, the door was shut.

TOGETHER.

Tick, tock, tick, tock, tick, tock,
  One, two, three, four, five, six!

SIXTH CHILD.

Six days we have in which to play.
  Six days to study and to work;
Six days there were when God did say,
  Let all the earth and heaven be made.

TOGETHER.

Tick, tock, tick, tock, tick, tock,
  One, two, three, four, five, six,
    Seven!

SEVENTH CHILD.

The seventh day the Lord did rest
  From all the work which he had done;
The Sabbath day by God was blest,
  And hallowed for his use alone.

TOGETHER.

Tick, tock, tick, tock, tick, tock,
  One, two, three, four, five, six,
    Seven, eight!

EIGHTH CHILD.

Eight souls were saved the ark within,
  So few there were who did believe
That God would surely punish sin,
  Only these eight would enter in.

TOGETHER.

Tick, tock, tick, tock, tick, tock,
  One, two, three, four, five, six,
    Seven, eight, nine!

NINTH CHILD.

"Where are the nine?" the Saviour said.
  "Were there not ten I did relieve?
Yet nine have quickly from me fled,
  And only one has thankful proved."

TOGETHER.

Tick, tock, tick, tock, tick, tock,
  One, two, three, four, five, six,
    Seven, eight, nine, ten!

TENTH CHILD.

Ten laws did God to Moses give,
  Ten laws which none have fully kept;
But Jesus died that we might live,
  He kept the law, and bore our sins.

TOGETHER.

Tick, tock, tick, tock, tick, tock,
One, two, three, four five, six,
  Seven, eight, nine, ten, eleven!

ELEVENTH CHILD.

Eleven disciples with Jesus alone,
  Twelve there were, but one had gone;
Eleven were true, false was one.
  May we be faithful to the end.

TOGETHER.

Tick, tock, tick, tock, tick, tock,
  One, two, three, four, five, six,
    Seven, eight, nine, ten, eleven, twelve!

TWELFTH CHILD.

Twelve months there are in every year,
  But the years are passing away;
Each tick of the clock cries to all here,
  To Jesus, oh, come, while 't is day.

MOTION SONG. *Lessons from the Clock.*
Page 13.

TOGETHER.

At the word *tick*, all right about face toward
the door of exit; at *tock*, march, keeping time
to the ticking movement, which keeps up, getting
fainter and fainter, till lost in the distance.

Tick, tock, tick, tock, etc.

CHILDREN'S DAY MATERIAL.

RESPONSIVE SERVICE FOR CHILDREN'S DAY.

TEACHER. The brook sings its low-voiced ripple, with now and then a little chatter as it meets and passes the stones. But underneath there is another voice. Meadow-Brook speaks to the blossoms : —

SCH. O all ye green things, things upon the earth, bless ye the Lord ; praise him and magnify him forever !

TEACHER. And bending Violet, Windflower, and Innocents softly respond : —

SCH. O ye waters that be above the firmament, bless ye the Lord : praise him and magnify him forever !

TEACHER. The Harebell rings its tiny joy bells : —

SCH. O be joyful in the Lord, all ye lands ; serve the Lord with gladness, and come before his presence with a song !

TEACHER. From far beyond and all around comes the universal chorus. The distant trees sing to the accompaniment of the wind-harp : —

SCH. O all ye winds of God, bless ye the Lord ; praise him and magnify him forever, stormy wind fulfilling his word !

TEACHER. And the wind-harp, touching its strings lightly, answers : —

SCH. For the Lord is a great God, and a great King above all gods !

TEACHER. The far-off mountains whisper to the low-hanging clouds : —

SCH. O ye lightnings and clouds, bless ye the Lord ; praise him and magnify him forever !

TEACHER. And the great, fleecy clouds reply : —

SCH. O ye mountains and hills, bless ye the Lord ; praise him and magnify him forever, for the strength of the hills is his also !

TEACHER. Then away far off the deep bass of the ocean sounds.

SCH. The sea is his and he made it : and his hands formed the dry land. O worship the Lord in the beauty of holiness ; let the whole earth stand in awe of him ; for he cometh, he cometh to judge the earth ; and with righteousness to judge the world and the people with his truth !

TEACHER. And the seagull bears the refrain far inland : —

SCH. We praise thee, O God ; we acknowledge thee to be the Lord. All the earth doth worship thee, the Father everlasting !

TEACHER. And back again in the inland meadows the gay-voiced bird and the yellow-coated bee join the great harmony : —

SCH. Praise ye the Lord ! The Lord's name be praised !

TEACHER. But a special voice comes to the listening, waiting children : —

SCH. O ye children of men, bless ye the Lord ; praise him, and magnify him forever ! Suffer little children and forbid them not, to come unto me, for of such is the kingdom of heaven.

                  — *Nature's Hallelujah.*

FLOWER OBJECT LESSON.

This may be recited by an older girl or boy. The bouquet needs to be arranged loosely, as follows : Lilies, white, also scarlet and yellow ; a full blown rose, a spray of lilies of the valley ; a branch of grapevine, fresh and green, another with moist roots clinging to it ; another branch wilted ; a bunch of fresh grasses, and a bunch of withered grasses and flowers. In the centre have an ear of corn in its yellow husk. In some available place covered from sight, have a little box, in which young corn is growing. This will need to be planted about three weeks before it is wanted. When the real flowers are not attainable, artificial ones will do.

(Place bouquet on table.) Lo, the winter is past; the rain is over and gone; the flowers appear on the earth; the fig tree putteth forth her green figs, and the vines with the tender grapes (take up the fresh grapevine), give a good smell. The vine shall give her fruit, and the ground shall give her increase, and the heaven shall give her dew.

(Take in the other hand a withered branch.) A branch cannot bear fruit of itself, except it abide in the vine. Jesus said, I am the vine, ye are the branches. He that abideth in me, and I in him (hold up fresh vine) the same bringeth forth much fruit.

(Lay these down and pick up the one with moist roots.) This was planted in a good soil, and by great waters, that it might bring forth branches, and that it might bear fruit, that it might be a goodly vine. The root of the righteous shall not be moved. Yea, they have taken root, they grow — yea, they bring forth fruit. The root of the righteous yieldeth fruit. The root of the righteous is a tree of life.

(Hold up in one hand the rose, and in the other the lilies of the valley.) I am the rose of Sharon and the lily of the valley.

(Take up bunch of lilies.) Why take ye thought for raiment? Consider the lilies how they grow; they toil not, neither do they spin: and yet I say unto you, that Solomon in all his glory was not arrayed like one of these.

(Pick up grasses.) And God said, Let the earth bring forth grass. (Hold it up.) And the tender grass sheweth itself. Thus saith the Lord that made thee, I will pour out my blessing upon thy offering, and they shall spring up as among the grass.

(Take up faded grass.) The sun is no sooner risen with a burning heat, but it withereth the grass, and the grace of the fashion of it perisheth. All flesh is grass; and all the goodliness thereof is as the flower of the field. (Take bunch of faded flowers in other hand, and hold both hands up in view of audience.) The grass withereth, the flower fadeth. (Lay them down.) As the flower of the grass he shall pass away.

(Hold up ear of corn.) Thou crownest the year with thy goodness. The valleys also are covered over with corn. The earth bringeth forth fruit, first the blade, then the ear, then the full corn in the ear. Like as a shock of corn cometh in his season, thou shalt come to thy grave. Except a corn of wheat fall into the ground and die, it abideth alone; but if it die, it bringeth forth much fruit. Thou sowest not that body which shall be, but bare grain. (Hold up a few separate kernels.) But God giveth it a body as it hath pleased him. (Throw back the cover which conceals the box of growing corn.) So is Christ risen from the dead, and is become the first fruits of them that slept. Even so, them also which sleep in Jesus, will God bring with him.

—Adapted from Pansy.

DAISIES, ROSEBUDS, AND PANSIES.

TWO CHILDREN.

Holding bunches of daisies.

We are little *Daisies*, waking into bloom,
Blessing by our sweetness all within the room.

TWO OTHERS.

With bunches of pansies.

We are little *Pansies*, each with cheerful face,
Smiling at the sunbeams, happy in God's grace.

TWO OTHERS.

Holding white and red rosebuds.

We are tiny *Rosebuds*, hiding in the green;
Don't we make a nosegay, nicest ever seen?

ALL.

Each child should hold flowers.

Daisies, Pansies, Rosebuds, little though we be,
We may trust in Jesus, and from sin be free.
We're our Father's flowers planted by his hand.
Will you tend and keep us for his heavenly land?

THE LITTLE BROWN SEED.

"I'm of no use," said a little brown seed;
  "Where shall I go and hide?
I'm little and brown, with nobody's love,
  And ugly beside."

So she rolled, and she rolled very quickly away,
  And tumbled on the ground;
The rain came in torrents, and fell upon her
  And all things around.

And she felt herself sinking in darkness beneath,
  Poor little faithless seed!
Where never an eye could see her sad fate,
  Oh, she was hidden indeed!

The little brown seed lay still in the earth,
  To herself still sighing,
Till at last with an effort she roused up and cried:
  "I'll begin by trying."

"I'll try and stop fretting, for 't is of no use,
  And if I've nobody's love,
I'll look up in hope, for there is One who will see,
  The dear God above."

Oh, would you believe it! straightway the dark ground
  Began to tremble and shake,
And make way for the little seed, hopeful now,
  Her upward way to take!

Up, up she went, till at last she saw
  The lovely, bright blue sky:
Oh, the beautiful spirit had found release,
  And the summer time was nigh!

The brightness and beauty that grew upon her
  I cannot begin to speak;
Crowned with flowers she stood, beloved by all,
  So lovely, yet so meek.
                                   — *Margaret Sidney.*

AUTUMN REUNION.

In schools where the members have been scattered during the summer, an autumn reunion is often the means of bringing all together again. Or with any school it may be made a bright Thanksgiving occasion. Trim the room with autumn leaves, goldenrod, crysanthemums, or other autumn flowers, also sheaves of wheat. Fruit and vegetables may be brought as offerings and afterwards sent to the sick or poor. Suggestions which may help in making up the program are given.
SONGS. *Autumn song.* Page 23. Praise Songs.
SCRIPTURE. Psalm 148 with motions. Praise Alphabet. Page 150.
RECITATIONS. As many of the following as are needed.

FOR THE GIVER.

What for the Giver, giant tree?
  "Fair gifts of gold and red —
These have I guarded patiently;
  Behold my fruit outspread!
From fragile buds it slowly grew,
Fed from his hands with crystal dew:
To thank him, at his feet I strew
  My gifts of gold and red."

What for the Giver, gentle flower?
  "My last look his shall be;
Has he not kept me, hour by hour, —
  Watched o'er me tenderly?
In gratitude for rain and shine,
And all the grace and beauty mine,
How could I fade and leave no sign?
  My last look his shall be."

What for the Giver, little one?
  Are there no gifts from thee?
Behold! the year is almost done,
  Must God still waiting be?
What deeds of kindness, flower-like, sweet?
What words, like songs, to ears they greet?
What heart fruits to lay at his feet? —
  Are there no gifts from thee?
                                   — *George Cooper.*

AUTUMN LEAVES.

(Three little boys and three little girls.)

FIRST GIRL.

With a wreath and branches of woodbine.

I have such lovely woodbine leaves,
  I like to look at them;
Is anything such pretty red
  In the New Jerusalem?

FIRST BOY

Responds by repeating Rev. 21: 19, 20.

SECOND GIRL.

I have a branch of yellow birch;
  I wonder if we 're told
Of anything so beautiful
  In the story dear and old?

SECOND BOY

Repeats Rev. 21: 2, 18.

THIRD GIRL.

And I have ferns as fresh and pure
  As spirit-ferns must be;
Is there any so beautiful
  In heaven, for us to see?

THIRD BOY

Repeats Rev. 21: 21.

FIRST GIRL.

But all these leaves will fade away,
  Till we just remember them;
Is there anything that will not die
  In the New Jerusalem?

ALL.

In concert.

"The grass withereth, the flower fadeth, but the word of the Lord endureth forever."

THE BIRDS' GOOD-BY.

" Where do you fly so fast,
    Pretty birds?
The meadows have lost their sheaves,
The wind through the woodland grieves,
  And the trees shower down
  Rich purple and brown,
Till I hardly tell you from the leaves,
    Little birds —
The beautiful, rustling leaves!"

" Will you forget us here,
    Pretty birds? —
The joys of the summer fair,
The brooks and the fragrant air?

When you wander afar,
 Where brighter lands are,
Will you dream of us pleasantly there,
   Little birds,
Though life is so happy there?"

" Have you no thought of fear,
    Pretty birds?
While winging across the sea,
Where shelterless you will be,
   When night lowers fast,
   And trumpets the blast,
Will you sigh for your home in the tree,
    Little birds,
Your soft swinging home in the tree?"

Sweetly they sang, " Good-by,
    Little child!
Though other lands may be bright,
'T is home gives the best delight!
And why need we fear?
The Father is near;
As he guideth your footsteps aright,
    Little child,
He guardeth our gentle flight!"
                            — *George Cooper.*

THE LEAVES OF THE TREES.

The pretty leaves are all gone from the trees. .
  Will they ever come again?
Yes, child: they will come with the spring's soft
   breeze,
  All fresh and beautiful then.

Where did they go — the leaves from the trees?
  And how will they grow again?
The old ones died, and to take their place
  The new will come bright and green.

And why did they die, the leaves of the trees?
  And how can the new ones grow?
Ah! little child, your questioning cease!
  Why and how we cannot know.

There is One who makes all the leaves of the trees,
  And counts them every one;
The hidden growth of each one he sees,
  And when its work is done.

The God above so good so great,
  In wisdom has made them all;
He knows when the buds for the spring to create,
  He knows when to let them fall.

And he who notes each tiny leaf
  Thinks also of you and me;
He watches our life, be it ever so brief,
  Though humble and troubled it be.

Then love him, and grow as the leaves of the trees
  In sunlight and dew and rain;
You know not how, but the way he sees,
  And you will not live in vain.
                        — *Mrs. Helen E. Brown.*

THE GLEANERS.

We are a little gleaning band;
  We cannot bind the sheaves,
But we can follow those who reap,
  And gather what each leaves.
We are not strong, but Jesus loves
  The weakest of the fold,
And in our feeble efforts proves
  His tenderness untold.

We are not rich; but we can give
  As we are passing on
A cup of water in his name
  To some poor, fainting one.
We are not wise, but Christ our Lord,
  Revealed to babes his will,
And we are sure from his dear Word
  He loves the children still.

We know that with our gathered grain
  Briers and leaves we bring;
Yet since we tried he smiles the same,
  And takes our offering.
Then let us still hosannas sing,
  As Christ doth conquering come,
Casting our treasures as he brings
  The heathen nations home.

THE FLIGHT OF THE BIRDS.

O wise little birds, how do you know
    The way to go
Southward and northward, to and fro?

Far up in the ether piped they:
  " We but obey
One who calleth us far away.

He calleth and calleth year by year,
    Now there, now here;
Ever he maketh the way appear."

Dear little birds, he calleth me
    Who calleth ye;
Would that I might as trusting be!

------◆------

CHRISTMAS SERVICE.

SONG. *Ring out. Merry Bells.* Page 31.
  TEACHER. What is this day?
  SCH. It is Christmas Day.

  TEACHER. Of what is Christmas Day to remind us?
  SCH. Of the birth of our Lord and Saviour,
Jesus Christ.

TEACHER. Was he really born on the twenty-fifth of December?

SCH. We do not know the exact day on which he was born.

TEACHER. Why then do we celebrate this day?

SCH. That there may be one special day on which we may all together think of the time when Jesus was born.

TEACHER. Where was Jesus born?

SCH. In Bethlehem of Judea.

TEACHER. Who had said this should be so?

SCH. God, through his prophet Micah.

TEACHER. How long was this spoken before Jesus was born?

SCH. More than 700 years.

TEACHER. To whom was the glad news first told?

SCH. To shepherds, keeping watch over their flock by night.

TEACHER. Who told them?

SCH. An angel.

TEACHER. In what words?

BOYS. "Fear not; for, behold, I bring you good tidings of great joy, which shall be to all people."

GIRLS. "For unto you is born this day in the city of David, a Saviour, which is Christ the Lord."

TEACHER. What had God's prophet Isaiah said of this child 700 years before?

SCH. "Unto us a child is born, unto us a Son is given."

TEACHER. What did Isaiah say this child should be called?

BOYS AND GIRLS ALTERNATELY. "His name shall be called Wonderful, Counsellor, The Mighty God, The Everlasting Father, The Prince of Peace."

TEACHER. What did the angel tell his mother, before his birth, to call his name?

SCH. "Thou shalt call his name Jesus; for he shall save his people from their sins."

TEACHER. By what other name did Isaiah say he should be called?

SCH. Em-man-u-el; which means, God with us.

TEACHER. What right had this babe to such a name?

SCH. He was God, and yet had come to be man with us.

TEACHER. What song did the angels who told the glad news to the shepherds sing?

SCH. "Glory to God in the highest, and on earth peace, good will toward men."

TEACHER. Let us also sing such a song : —

MOTION SONG. *Ringing for Jesus.* Page 42.

PRAYER.

THE FIRST CHRISTMAS MORNING.

The questions may be asked by single voices, the passages of Scripture in the Old and New Testaments alternately being given in turn by girls and boys, or by two classes. Or, six girls and six boys may be ranged in two semi circles, opposite each other, speaking in the manner designated below.

FIRST BOY.

Come, children, now, and let us see,
   This gladsome Christmas morning,
Whether you know the reason we
   Rejoice on Christmas morning.
What saith the prophet? From whose stem
Should a Rod to bless the sons of men
   Come forth on Christmas morning?

GIRLS, IN CONCERT. "And there shall come forth a rod out of the stem of Jesse, and a branch shall grow out of his roots." (Is. 11:1.)

SIXTH GIRL.

Seven hundred years must pass away
   Ere came that Christmas morning;
And *was* the Babe born on that day,
   That best-loved Christmas morning,
Branch that from Jesse's roots should grow,
The Rod that from his stem should blow,
   Forth on that Christmas morning?

BOYS, IN CONCERT. "I have found David the son of Jesse a man after mine own heart, which shall fulfil all my will. Of this man's seed hath God according to his promise raised unto Israel a Saviour, Jesus." (Acts 13: 22, 23.)

SECOND BOY.

Speaks the prophet to us again
   About that Christmas morning?
Telleth he what shall be the *name*,
   That blessed Christmas morning,
Given to him who should be born
On that bright, that glorious morn,
   Most glorious Christmas morning?

GIRLS, IN CONCERT. "For unto us a child is born, unto us a son is given; and the government shall be upon his shoulder; and his name shall be called Wonderful, Counsellor, The Mighty God, The Everlasting Father, The Prince of Peace." (Is. 9: 6.)

FIFTH GIRL.

Boys, can you tell what was the name,
   Before that Christmas morning,
The angel, who to Mary came
   And promised Christmas morning,
Did give to him before his birth?
The sweetest name e'er heard on earth,
   First born on Christmas morning.

BOYS, IN CONCERT. "Thou shalt call his name Jesus, for he shall save his people from their sins." (Matt. 1: 21.)

THIRD BOY.

When the news in heaven was told,
　About that Christmas morning,
When e'en in heaven the echoes rolled
　Of coming Christmas morning,
In angel hearts what feelings stirred
When first the wondrous news they heard,
　There should be Christmas morning?

GIRLS, IN CONCERT. "The morning stars sang together, and all the sons of God shouted for joy." (Job 38: 7.)

FOURTH GIRL.

If heaven itself did ring with joy,
　Upon that Christmas morning,
Gladness mixed with no alloy,
　That happy Christmas morning;
Could any from that shining host
Be spared, to shout unto earth's lost,
　"'T is come! The Christmas morning"?

BOYS, IN CONCERT. "And lo! the angel of the Lord came upon them, and the glory of the Lord shone round about them. And suddenly there was with the angel a multitude of the heavenly host." (Luke 2: 9, 13.)

FOURTH BOY.

When heaven with glad music rang,
　To herald Christmas morning,
Angels and stars together sang
　Songs of Christmas morning;
Whom in the songs they there did raise,
Whom did those heavenly angels praise
　For sending Christmas morning?

GIRLS, IN CONCERT. "Not unto us, O Lord, not unto us, but unto thy name give glory, for thy mercy and for thy truth's sake." (Ps. 115: 1.)

THIRD GIRL.

When on Bethlehem's field that night,
　Ere dawned the Christmas morning,
The glory of the Lord shone bright,
　Ushering in Christmas morning,
How did the angelic host rejoice,
Praising God with heart and voice,
　Until the Christmas morning?

BOYS, IN CONCERT. "Glory to God in tne highest, and on earth peace, good will toward men." (Luke 2: 14.)

FIFTH BOY.

Prophets and sages all foretold
　That precious Christmas morning;
The prophet Micah did unfold
　Where, on that Christmas morning,
The promised Saviour should be found.
Where was that place, hence holy ground,
　Honored with Christmas morning?

GIRLS, IN CONCERT. "But thou, Bethlehem Ephratah, though thou be little among the thousands of Judah, yet out of thee shall he come forth unto me that is to be ruler in Israel." (Micah 5: 2.)

SECOND GIRL.

And when the years had rolled away
　That held the Christmas morning,
The night before that glorious day,
　Which brought our Christmas morning,
What said the angels to the men
Who watched their flocks near Bethlehem,
　Night before Christmas morning?

BOYS, IN CONCERT. "Fear not, for behold, I bring you good tidings of great joy, which shall be to all people. For unto you is born this day in the city of David, a Saviour, which is Christ the Lord." (Luke 2: 10, 11.)

SIXTH BOY.

'T was fourteen hundred years and more
　Before that Christmas morning
That wicked Balaam, son of Beor,
　Dreamed of that Christmas morning.
What did he say of Jacob's star
And sceptre, which should stretch afar,
　E'en down to Christmas morning?

GIRLS, IN CONCERT. "I shall see him, but not now; I shall behold him, but not nigh; there shall come a star out of Jacob, and a sceptre shall rise out of Israel." (Num. 24: 17.)

FIRST GIRL.

And after all the lapse of ages,
　At last dawned Christmas morning;
When to King Herod, Eastern sages
　Came on that Christmas morning,
What said they of that wondrous star
Whose light they followed from afar,
　Westward till Christmas morning?

BOYS, IN CONCERT. "Where is he that is born King of the Jews? for we have seen his star in the east, and are come to worship him." (Matt. 2: 2.)

GIRLS, IN CONCERT.

And now we'll tell why girl and boy
　Are glad on Christmas morning.
To us that tidings of great joy
　Was brought on Christmas morning:
Rejoice! for us the incarnate Word,
A Saviour, which is Christ the Lord,
　Was born on Christmas morning.

BOYS, IN CONCERT.

Shout, children, shout the glad story,
　Clust'ring round Christmas morning;
How the Lord, the Lord of glory,
　Came down on Christmas morning.
Then let us, like the angelic host,
Praise Father, Son, and Holy Ghost,
　Who gave us Christmas morning.

GIRLS. "Glory to God in the highest, and on earth peace, good will toward men." (Luke 2: 14.)

BOYS REPEAT. "Glory to God," etc.

GIRLS AND BOYS TOGETHER. "Glory," etc.

M. G. K.

BETTER STILL.

A CHRISTMAS RECITATION FOR FOUR CHILDREN.

[*Written for Teacher's Edition, Children's Quarterly.*]

FIRST BOY.

I wonder if a little boy
 About as big as I,
Was in the field that blessed time
 When angels filled the sky?
Perhaps, close cuddling by his side,
 His pretty pet lamb lay,
And both were wrapt in slumber while
 The night-watch wore away.
I wish that I had been there too,
 Among the shepherd band,
And wakened from my dreams to hear
 That chorus sweet and grand!

SECOND BOY.

Yes, so do I! I would have borne
 The lamb upon my arm,
And with the older shepherds gone
 (Beneath the starlight calm),
To where the holy Christ-child lay
 Asleep upon a bed of hay.

FIRST GIRL.

He was the precious Lamb of God;
 He'll take our sins away,
If trustfully we come to him,
 This very Christmas day.
He is the tender shepherd too,
 Who gathers to his breast
The children who will be his lambs,
 So happy, and so blest.

SECOND GIRL.

We, more than Bethlehem's shepherds know
Of this dear Friend who loves us so;
Then let us in his beauty grow,
And tell the joyful word anew
That Jesus came to save us too.
I think this better still — don't you? —
Than if we'd been there long ago,
And seen the midnight sky aglow.
The angel song is in our hearts,
The heavenly glory ne'er departs,
When Jesus is our Dayspring bright,
Our joy, our song, our living Light.

E. E. Hewitt.

WHY WE LOVE TO BRING CHRISTMAS GIFTS FOR JESUS.

GRACE.

I've been thinking, little sisters, if a heathen child
 should be
Hither brought from some lone islet in the far-off
 Southern sea,
And should ask why summer garlands deck our
 house this festive day,
Why we seem so glad and happy, Annie dear,
 what would you say?

ANNIE.

I would tell the lovely story of the Babe of
 Bethlehem —
How they laid him in a manger when by night
 he came to them;
I would tell how Mary dressed him, and with soft
 and fragrant hay,
I think, the manger bed she made where baby
 Jesus lay.

FANNIE.

I would tell that gentle shepherds, watching o'er
 their flocks by night,
Saw suddenly around them the shining glory
 light,
And heard the angel's tidings about the Saviour's
 birth;
And then the heavenly chorus, " Good-will and
 peace on earth."

BESSIE.

I would tell the wondrous story about the shin-
 ing star
That led the holy wise men from Eastern lands
 afar,
Until they found sweet Mary and the Jesus-child
 with her,
And gave him costly presents — gold, frankin-
 cense, and myrrh.

CARRIE.

Then I would tell how Jesus, this blessed little
 Child,
Grew up to perfect manhood, holy, pure, and
 undefiled;
How, living, serving, dying, himself for us he
 gave;
He loved us so, he lived and died from sin and
 shame to save.

NETTIE.

Then to the little heathen child I think that I
 would say :
"Don't you think that we have shown you why
 we love the Christmas Day?
Don't you see we must be happy, and our happy
 gladness show,
Upon the birthday of the One who blessed and
 loved us so?"

SADIE.

And then we all would promise the heathen child
 that we
Will send the knowledge of his love to the islands
 of the sea.
Till all the world shall hear of him who came in
 lowly birth,
Whose love, in God's good time, shall bring good-
 will on all the earth.

TEACHER. The shepherds and the wise men
all brought offerings. We know much more of
the Saviour King than they did; what shall we
bring him to-day?

(If gifts have been brought by the children, let the object be clearly stated, and the gifts brought up. If the offering is *money*, a pretty way is to enclose it in little bags of bright-colored silesia, which may be hung on a tree, surely beautiful fruit for the King.)

Follow the offering by a brief prayer giving them to Christ our King.

TEACHER. What offerings that are very real, yet that cannot be seen by *our* eyes, can children offer to the Saviour King?

THE CHILDREN'S OFFERING.

For six children.

FIRST CHILD.

I'll give my *heart* to Jesus,
  In childhood's tender spring;
I know that he will not despise
  So small an offering.

SECOND CHILD.

I'll give my *soul* to Jesus,
  And calmly, gladly rest
Its youthful hope and fond desires
  Upon his loving breast.

THIRD CHILD.

I'll give my *mind* to Jesus,
  And seek in thoughtful hours
His Spirit's grace to consecrate
  Its early opening powers.

FOURTH CHILD.

I'll give my *strength* to Jesus,
  Of foot and hand and will;
Run where he sends, and ever strive
  His pleasure to fulfil.

FIFTH CHILD.

I'll give my *time* to Jesus,
  Oh, that each hour might be
Filled up with holy love for him,
  Who spent his life for me!

SIXTH CHILD.

I'll give my *wealth* to Jesus, —
  'Tis little I possess;
But all I am, and all I have,
  Dear Lord, accept and bless.

SINGING.

PARTING WORDS.

SCH. **Thanks be unto God for his unspeakable gift.** (2 Cor. 9:15.)

TEACHER. Blessing, and honour, and glory, and power, be unto him that sitteth upon the throne, and unto the Lamb, forever and ever. (Rev. 5:13.)

ALL. **The grace of our Lord Jesus Christ, be with you all. Amen.**

WISHES.

FIRST CHILD, HOLDING A GILT STAR.

I wish I were a little *star*,
  I'd shine, I'd shine for Jesus;
E'en little rays can reach afar,
  And some one seeing it might try
  To gain the heavenly home on high,
And then there'd be another star
  To shine, to shine for Jesus.

SECOND CHILD, HOLDING CANDLE OR LITTLE LAMP.

I'd like to be a little *light*,
  To glow, to glow for Jesus;
Perhaps he'd make me shine so bright,
  Some little friend might see the way
  That leads to Christ and endless day,
And be himself a little light,
  And burn so bright for Jesus.

THIRD CHILD, HOLDING STUFFED BIRD.

I wish I were a little *bird*,
  I'd sing, I'd sing for Jesus
The sweetest things ear ever heard;
  I'd sing of all his loving ways,
  My voice I'd raise in songs of praise,
Sure never yet did little bird
  Thus sing, thus sing for Jesus.

FOURTH CHILD, HOLDING FLOWER.

I wish I were a little *flower*,
  To bloom, to bloom for Jesus;
I'd cheer some sad heart every hour;
  For though I grew so near the ground
  I could shed sweetness all around;
For thus it is a little flower,
  May bloom, may bloom for Jesus.

FIFTH CHILD, WITH BRANCH OF EVERGREEN.

I wish I were a tall, *green tree*,
  To bear good fruit for Jesus,
Rooted in love I'd like to be;
  Then leaf and branch and blossom fair,
  And ripened fruit, both rich and rare,
And rest and shelter 'neath my tree —
  All these I'd give for Jesus.

SIXTH CHILD, A LITTLE GIRL.

I'd rather be a little *girl*,
  And work, and work for Jesus.
Sure, he who made the little pearl,
  To gleam unseen beneath the sea,
  Would welcome e'en a child like me,
Or any other little girl
  To work, to work for Jesus.

SEVENTH CHILD, A LITTLE BOY:
I'm glad I am a little *boy*,
  To try to grow like Jesus;
I wish you all could know the joy
  Of serving him who for us died,
  Who for our sins was crucified.
Come, every girl and every boy,
  And live and live for Jesus.

ALL, IN CONCERT.
To be a child is better far,
Than bird or flower or tree or star.
We have undying souls to save,
Which birds, and trees, and stars don't have.

FIRST CHILD.
And yet for Jesus I may *shine*,

FOURTH CHILD.
A *flower's* sweetness may be mine,

SECOND CHILD.
And I can *show* some friend the way,

THIRD CHILD.
While I can *sing* his praise each day,

FIFTH CHILD.
Ripe fruit of *love* for him I'll bear,

SIXTH CHILD.
What e'er I can shall be my share,

SEVENTH CHILD.
And thus we all will do our part

ALL.
With ready hand and willing heart,
To show our love for Jesus.
                                   M. G. K.

BIBLE ALPHABETS.

AN ALPHABET OF PRAISE.

All thy works shall praise thee, O Lord. (Ps. 145:10.)
Bless the Lord, O my soul. (Ps. 103:2.)
Come let us sing unto the Lord. (Ps. 95:1.)
Declare his glory among the heathen, his wonders among all people. (Ps. 96:3.)
Enter into his gate with thanksgiving. (Ps. 100:4.)
Forget not all his benefits. (Ps. 103:2.)
Great is the Lord and greatly to be praised. (Ps. 145:3.)
He giveth to the beast his food. (Ps. 147:9.)
I will praise thee, O Lord, among the people. (Ps. 108:3.)
Just and true are thy ways. (Rev. 15:3.)
Know ye that the Lord he is God; it is he that hath made us and not we ourselves. (Ps. 100:3.)
Let every thing that hath breath praise the Lord. (Ps. 150:6.)
My mouth shall speak the praise of the Lord. (Ps. 145:21.)
Not unto us, O Lord, not unto us, but unto thy name give glory. (Ps. 115:1.)
O give thanks unto the Lord, for he is good. (Ps. 118:1.)
Praise him for his mighty acts. (Ps. 150:2.)
Remember his marvellous works that he hath done. (Ps. 105:5.)
Serve the Lord with gladness. (Ps. 100:2.)
The Lord hath done great things for us; whereof we are glad. (Ps. 126:3.)
Unto thee, O God, do we give thanks. (Ps. 75:1.
While I live will I praise thee. (Ps. 146:2.)
Young men and maidens, old men and children, let them praise the name of the Lord. (Ps. 148:12, 13.)
                                   M. G. K.

AN ALPHABET OF BIBLE PRAYERS.

Abide with us. (Luke 24:29.)
Bless me, even me also, O my Father. (Gen. 27:38.)
Create in me a clean heart, O God. (Ps. 51:10.)
Deliver my soul, O Lord, from lying lips, and from a deceitful tongue. (Ps. 120:2.)
Evermore give us this bread. (John 6:34.)
Forgive all my sins. (Ps. 25:18.)
God be merciful to me a sinner. (Luke 18:13.)
Hide me under the shadow of thy wings. (Ps. 17:8.)
I am thine, save me. (Ps. 119:94.)
Jesus, Master, have mercy on us. (Luke 17:13.)
Keep the door of my lips. (Ps. 141:3.)
Lord, teach us to pray. (Luke 11:1.)
Make me to go in the path of thy commandments. (Ps. 119:35.)
Not my will but thine be done. (Luke 2:42.)
Open thou mine eyes, that I may behold wondrous things out of thy Law. (Ps. 119:18.)
Plead my cause, O Lord. (Ps. 35:1.)
Quicken me, O Lord, for thy name's sake. (Ps. 143:11.)
Remember me. (Luke 23:42.)
Set a watch, O Lord, before my mouth. (Ps. 141:3.)
Teach me to do thy will. (Ps. 143:10.)
Uphold me according to thy word. (Ps. 119:116.)
Wash me and I shall be whiter than snow. (Ps. 51:7.)
Yea, let none that wait on thee be ashamed. (Ps. 25:3.)
                                   M. G. K.

AN ALPHABET OF BIBLE PROMISES.

A new heart also will I give you. and a new spirit will I put within you. (Ezek. 36: 26.)

Believe on the Lord Jesus Christ and thou shalt be saved. (Acts 16: 31.)

Come unto me all ye that labor and are heavy laden and I will give you rest. (Matt. 11: 28.)

Draw nigh to God, and he will draw nigh to thee. (Jas. 4: 8.)

Eye hath not seen, nor ear heard, neither have entered into the heart of man, the things which God hath prepared for them that love him. (1 Cor. 2: 9.)

Fear not, for I am with thee. (Isa. 43: 5.)

Give and it shall be given unto you. Luke 6: 38.

Him that cometh unto me, I will in no wise cast out. (John 6: 37.)

I will never leave thee, nor forsake thee. (Heb. 13: 5.)

Jesus' last promise is — Lo, I am with you alway. (Matt. 28: 20.)

Knock and it shall be opened unto you. (Matt. 7: 7.)

Like as a father pitieth his children, so the Lord pitieth them that fear him. (Psa. 103: 13.)

My grace is sufficient for thee. (2 Cor. 1: 29.)

Now therefore go, and I will be with thy mouth to teach thee. (Ex. 4: 12.)

Open thy mouth wide and I will fill it. (Ps. 81: 10.)

Peace I leave with you, my peace I give unto you. (John 14: 27.)

In quietness and in confidence shall be your strength. (Is. 30: 15.)

Resist the devil and he will flee from you. (Jas. 4: 7.)

Seek and ye shall find. (Matt. 7: 7.)

The blood of Jesus Christ his Son cleanseth us from all sin. (1 John 1: 7.)

Unto you is born this day in the city of David a Saviour which is Christ the Lord. (Luke 2: 11.)

Verily verily I say unto you, Whatsoever you shall ask the Father in my name he will give it you. (John 16: 23.)

Whosoever calleth on the name of the Lord shall be saved. (Acts 221.)

Ye are my friends if ye do whatsoever I command you. (John 15: 14.)

AN ALPHABET OF BIBLE COMMANDS.

Abhor that which is evil.

Be ye kind to one another.

Cease to do evil and learn to do well.

Do good and sin not.

Enter not into temptation.

Fear God and keep his commandments.

Glorify God at all times.

Honor thy father and thy mother.

In everything give thanks.

Judge not.

Keep thy tongue from evil.

Little children, love one another.

My son, give me thine heart.

No man can serve two masters.

Obey your parents.

Pray without ceasing.

Quench not the Spirit.

Remember now thy Creator.

Speak the truth.

Trust ye in the Lord forever.

Verily I say unto you he that believeth on me hath everlasting life.

Watch and pray.

Yield yourself to God.

B. F. V.

Motto exercises may be formed by changing the order of these commands, as GOD IS LOVE.

HEALTH ALPHABET FOR INDUSTRIAL SCHOOLS.

There are some things we need to be told over and over, and a different version helps to give emphasis. The alphabetical "pegs" may also serve to fasten the following wise rules in our memories.

As soon as you are up, shake blankets and sheets:

Better be without shoes than sit with wet feet;

Children, if healthy, are active, not still;

Damp beds and damp clothes will both make you ill:

Eat slowly, and always chew your food well;

Freshen the air in the house where you dwell;

Garments must never be made to be tight;

Homes will be healthy if airy and light.

If you wish to be well, as you do, I've no doubt,

Just open the windows before you go out;

Keep your rooms always tidy and clean —

Let dust on the furniture never be seen;

Much illness is caused by the want of pure air —

Now to open your windows be ever your care.

Old rags and old rubbish should never be kept;

People should see that their floors are well swept.

Quick movements in children are healthy and right;

Remember the young cannot thrive without light.

See that the cistern is clean to the brim;

Take care that your dress is all tidy and trim;

Use your nose to find out if there be a bad drain —

Very sad are the fevers that come in its train.

Walk as much as you can without feeling fatigue;

Xerxes could walk full many a league.

Your health is your wealth, which your wisdom must keep;

Zeal will help a good cause, and the good you will reap.

THE CHILD'S DAY.

MOTTO:—ALL MY HOURS FOR JESUS.

The hands of the clock may be set at different hours for the Child's Day; or this may be taught a part at a time to vary the Primary program.

AWAKING.

I laid me down and slept; I awaked; for the Lord sustained me. (Ps. 3:5.)

Day again is dawning, darkness flies away,
Now from sleep awaking, let me rise and pray:
Jesus! tender Shepherd, watching while I slept,
Bless the little lambkin Thou hast safely kept.

Thou hast prepared the light and the sun. (Ps. 74:16.)

PRAYING.

In the morning I will direct my prayer unto thee. (Ps. 5:3.)

Now I wake and see the light;
'T is God has kept me through the night—
To him I lift my hands and pray
That he would keep me through the day;
And if I die before 't is done,
Great God, accept me through thy Son.

Those that seek me early shall find me. (Prov. 8:17.)

WASHING.

Wash me thoroughly from mine iniquity, and cleanse me from my sin. (Ps. 51:2.)

I bring my sins to Jesus,
To wash my crimson stains
White in his blood most precious,
Till not a spot remains.

Lord, if thou wilt, thou canst make me clean. (Luke 5:12.)

DRESSING.

Let thy garments be always white. (Eccles. 9:8.)

With loving hands our bodies dress,
And fitting garments please us,
We'll think of Christ, our Righteousness,
Our snow white robe, our Jesus.

BREAKFASTING.

Whether, therefore, ye eat, or drink, or whatsoever ye do, do all to the glory of God. (1 Cor. 10:31.)

Let us with a joyful mind,
Praise the Lord for he is kind.
All things living he doth feed,
His full hand supplies our need.
All we eat, and drink, and wear,
Proves our Heavenly Father's care.

Who giveth food to all flesh; for his mercy endureth forever. (Ps. 136:25.)

STUDYING.

Learn of me. (Matt. 11:29.)

While we look within thy word,
Show thy grace to us, O Lord;
In these pages may we see
Every lesson point to thee.

Teach me thy way, O Lord. (Ps. 27:11.)

DINING.

Feed me with food convenient for me. (Prov. 30:8.)

Our kind heavenly Father,
By whom we all are fed,
Thanks to thee for home and friends,
And thanks for daily bread.

Jesus said, "My meat is to do the will of him that sent me." (John 4:34.)

WORKING.

If any would not work, neither should he eat. (2 Thess. 3:10.)

With willing heart and hand,
Your daily task pursue,
Work, for the day wears on,
Ask, "What will Jesus do?"

Whatsoever thy hand findeth to do, do it with thy might. (Eccles. 9:10.)

PLAYING.

Love one another. (1 John 3:11.)

In active work, in healthful play,
When all things smile and please us,
We'll find him near, our strength and stay,
Our loving friend, our Jesus.

Whatsoever ye would that men should do to you, do ye even so to them. (Matt. 7:12.)

SINGING.

Sing unto the Lord with thanksgiving. (Ps. 147:7.)

Saviour, blessed Saviour,
Listen while we sing,
Hearts and voices raising
Praises to our King.

Singing with grace in your hearts to the Lord. (Col. 3:16.)

PRAYING.

Evening and morning, and at noon will I pray.
(Ps. 55:17.)

> Glory to thee, my God, this night,
> For all the blessings of the light;
> Keep me, Oh, keep me, King of kings,
> Under the shadow of thy wings.

Whatsoever ye shall ask in prayer believing,
ye shall receive. (Matt. 21:22.)

BEDTIME.

I will both lay me down in peace and sleep;
for thou Lord, only makest me dwell in safety.
(Ps. 4:8.)

He will take care of you; all through the night,
Jesus the Shepherd, his little one keeps;
Darkness to him is the same as the light.
He never slumbers, and he never sleeps.

He that keepeth thee, will not slumber. (Ps.
121:3.)

M. G. K.

THE CHILD'S WEEK.

SUNDAY.

MORNING.

This is the day which the Lord hath made; we
will rejoice and be glad in it. (Ps. 118:24.)

O let me be thoughtful and prayerful to-day,
And not spend a minute in trifling or play;
Remember these Sabbaths were graciously given,
To teach me to seek, and prepare me for heaven.

EVENING.

Remember the Sabbath day to keep it holy.
(Ex. 20:8.)

MONDAY.

MORNING.

The blood of Jesus Christ his Son cleanseth
us from all sin. (1 John 1:7.)

> At his feet confess your sin,
> Seek forgiveness there,
> For his blood can make you clean,
> He will hear your prayer.

EVENING.

Wash me and I shall be whiter than snow.
(Ps. 51:7.)

TUESDAY.

MORNING.

Who loved me, and gave himself for me. (Gal.
2:20.)

> Saviour, teach me day by day,
> Love's sweet lesson to obey;
> Sweeter lesson cannot be,
> Loving him who first loved me.

EVENING.

Love one another as I have loved you. (John
15:12.)

WEDNESDAY.

MORNING.

Keep thy tongue from evil. (Ps. 34:13.)

> Ear and eye and tongue,
> Guard while thou art young;
> For, alas! those busy three
> Can unruly members be.

EVENING.

Set a watch, O Lord, before the door of my
mouth; keep the door of my lips. (Ps. 141:3.)

THURSDAY.

MORNING.

And will watch to see what he will say unto
me. (Hab. 2:11.)

> Master, speak and make me ready,
> When thy voice is truly heard,
> With obedience glad and steady,
> Still to follow every word.
> I am listening, Lord, for thee;
> Master, speak, Oh, speak to me!

EVENING.

Whatsoever he saith unto you, do it. (John
2:5.)

FRIDAY.

MORNING.

And went and told Jesus. (Matt. 14:12.)

> Little ones are often sorry
> For the naughty things they do;
> Troubles reach us all, and worry
> Little hearts and big ones too.
> Then tell Jesus,
> That's the best thing you can do.

EVENING.

If ye shall ask anything in my name, I will do
it. (John 14:14.)

SATURDAY.

MORNING.

Whatsoever ye do, do it heartily, as to the
Lord. (Col. 3:23.)

> Up and doing, little children,
> Up and doing while 't is day;
> Do the work the Master gives you,
> Do not linger by the way.
> For we all have work before us;
> You, dear child, as well as I—
> Let us seek to learn our duty,
> And to do it heartily.

EVENING.

Lord, what wilt thou have me to do? (Acts
9:6.)

NEW YEAR'S EVE.

Tell me, little Mabel, with your face against the pane,
What is it you are watching 'mid the darkness and the rain?
I was only trying, peering in the darkness so,
Whether I could see the years, as past they come and go.

Darling little Mabel, with such wistful eyes and gaze,
Do you really think to see them separate their ways?

Oh yes! The children told me that it was surely true,
If we watched to-night, we'd see the meeting 'twixt the two.
But I'm afraid that so hard it does both rain and snow,
That we cannot see the New Year come, neither the old one go.

Dearest little Mabel, come and rest your head on me,
And tell me what it was you expected thus to see.

Oh, I thought the Old Year must be very, very old;
Since he came, so long ago, thousands of hours have rolled.
He must be very weary with the work that he has done,
For he has never rested a day since he begun.
Mamma, how I wonder whether what I thought was snow
Were his locks of hoary hair? Oh, how I'd like to know!
Perhaps he stripped the leaves from trees that once were green,
That he might find a cane so strong his falt'ring steps 't would screen.
Mamma, dear mamma, hark! how loud the wind is crying!
Do you think it is because the Old Year now lies dying?

Mamma's little Mabel, God will shield us from all harm;
Tell me the rest, my darling, sheltered by this loving arm.

I thought surely a white angel would have come
And taken him in his bosom before the dark begun;
Perhaps we did not hear him, they are are such noiseless things;
And what we thought was snow were feathers from his wings.
I hope they will carry him gently, like a little child,
And lay him down to rest, for it's a darksome night and wild.
Dear Old Year! now that your work is done, are you glad to die?
Or do you want to grow young, like the year that's coming by?
Is every month your wife, and the weeks your children dear?
The days their daughters? Then the hours that seem never here,
And the swift-winged minutes, dear Old Year, tell me what are they?
Don't die just yet, Old Year! wait a minute while you say.

Loving little Mabel, tell me what was in your heart
About the bright young New Year, who now must take his part.

I know sweet glad young New Year must be very tiny;
Through the trees we soon shall see his silvery robes so shiny.
Dear little thing! Old Year ought to wait a day or two,
On purpose to show New Year what he has got to do.
I'm afraid that he grew cruel as he was growing old,
And will leave the little darling right out there in the cold.
I should think angels would come and hold his little head —
Perhaps when we thought it snowed they were making up his bed.
Or 'twas to soften the hard ground that he might learn to walk,
For I suppose the New Year can neither walk nor talk.
I wish Spring-time were here with her beautiful flowers,
They're prettier playthings for him than these icicle-showers.
I wonder whether the angels will sing him to sleep,
Or whether dying Old Year will stand o'er him and weep.

Mamma, dear mamma, hark! how loud the wind is crying!
Do you think it is because the Old Year now lies dying?
Mamma, must there come a time when the New Year too must die?
What was that? I thought I heard the years go passing by!

Precious little Mabel, sleeping sweetly on my breast;
Holy angels guard my darling, watching o'er her rest.
Guard my sweetest, choicest treasure, sent me from the skies,
For what we call our Mabel is an angel in disguise.

— M. G. Kennedy.

LILY'S CHRISTMAS GIFTS.

FOR A VERY LITTLE GIRL.

Each time a *kiss* is mentioned, she *throws kisses*. At "*Hurrah*," she waves her handkerchief.

A very little maid am I,
  Of money I have none to spare;
But each to give some gift I'll try —
  I'm sure you all will like your share.

My gifts I'm sure you wish will fit;
  That they will please you well I know.
Dear pastor, over where you sit,
  Take my first gift — this kiss I throw.

Here's a sweet kiss for teacher kind,
  For I love once in every week
Her in our schoolroom here to find,
  While she of Jesus' love does speak.

I'll not forget those friends who cheer
Our hearts this anniversary night,

And by their welcome presence here
  Add joy and beauty to the sight.

No, no, dear friends; you love us so,
  To slight you thus will never do.
A kiss for every one I'll throw,
  Quick! catch them! you! and you! and you!

And here's our superintendent's kiss,
  Hold out your hands and catch it now;
You surely will not like to miss
  This chance of making your best bow.

Hurrah, for Christmas time is here!
  Hurrah, hurrah, with all your might!
I wish you all a Happy New Year!
  And kiss you all once more. Good-night.

M. G. K.

INDEX OF SUBJECTS.

SONGS.

SERVICES, ETC.